The Blind Scientist

The Blind Scientist

Unmasking the Misguided Methodology
of Neo-Darwinism

Alexander J. Bonitto
WITH John S. Knox

FOREWORD BY
Brian M. Kelley

WIPF & STOCK · Eugene, Oregon

THE BLIND SCIENTIST
Unmasking the Misguided Methodology of Neo-Darwinism

Copyright © 2024 Alexander J. Bonitto and John S. Knox. All rights reserved. Except for brief quotations in critical publications or reviews, no part of this book may be reproduced in any manner without prior written permission from the publisher. Write: Permissions, Wipf and Stock Publishers, 199 W. 8th Ave., Suite 3, Eugene, OR 97401.

Wipf & Stock
An Imprint of Wipf and Stock Publishers
199 W. 8th Ave., Suite 3
Eugene, OR 97401

www.wipfandstock.com

PAPERBACK ISBN: 978-1-6667-8317-9
HARDCOVER ISBN: 978-1-6667-8318-6
EBOOK ISBN: 978-1-6667-8319-3

VERSION NUMBER 03/01/24

Unless otherwise noted, scriptures are taken from the THE HOLY BIBLE, ENGLISH STANDARD VERSION (ESV): Scriptures taken from THE HOLY BIBLE, ENGLISH STANDARD VERSION ® Copyright© 2001 by Crossway, a publishing ministry of Good News Publishers. Used by permission.

"But test everything; hold fast what is good" (1 Thess 5:21 ESV).

Contents

List of Illustrations | viii
Foreword by Brian M. Kelley | ix
Preface | xv
Acknowledgements | xix

1 The Relationship Between Science and Facts | 1
2 A Summary of Neo-Darwinian Scholarship | 12
3 A Careful Consideration of Methodological Approach | 35
4 Putting Neo-Darwinism to the Test | 40
5 Neo-Darwinism and Christian Apologetics | 79
6 Implications, Discussions, and Solutions for Neo-Darwinian Limitations | 90

Bibliography | 101
Index | 107

List of Illustrations

Figure 1 | 22
Figure 2 | 25
Figure 3 | 34
Figure 4 | 44

Foreword

IT CAN BE EASILY argued that (historically) people who had money ruled the world. To wit, the world's golden rule is that those with the gold make the rules. Money translates into power, power into control, and control into oppression. More recently—especially with the development of the internet and internet-enabled smart devices, there has been a shift in this axiom to add intellectual substance to money-based decision-making. Now, data translates into money so that people with the data rule the world. Look at industries with the most rapid growth and influence; all of them are about data. Nearly all internet-based activities—especially social media—are about gathering, manipulating, and controlling information, and nowhere is this more impactful than within the sciences.

The entire foundation of science is based upon questioning, hypothesizing, testing, replicating, and debating. Scientific advances depend on these cyclical and dynamic activities, which is why authentic scientists rarely, if ever, speak in absolutes because science rarely, if ever, produces absolutes. When even the most rigorous of the sciences are discussed in terms of statistics, and the foundation of statistics is of probability, and probabilities are never 100 percent, then scientific conclusions should be presented in the context of process and probability as well as with pessimism.

Pessimism is best addressed by replication and debate, and this is exactly what is being suppressed. To that end, for thoughtful scientists, the science is never settled. Furthermore, people are being told to follow the science, trust the science, and comply with the science, in the absence of any transparency or debate. Often, just the opposite is the status quo as debate is met with hostility and retribution as well as "cancelling." In fact, we are told not to question the science which is the antithesis of science.

As soon as this becomes the prevailing approach and reality, then all science becomes political science. The freedoms many come to enjoy are being rapidly eroded by the premise of scientific absolutes. Data is the new gold and data mining is the new highly sought-after occupation.

The bombardment of scientific "truths" is overwhelming, especially when so few people actually understand science as a process, product, or profession. Clearly, humanity benefits from science, and people can see those benefits all around us in nearly every sector—transportation, healthcare, education, communication, entertainment, and technology. It is because of these amazing successes that people can be so easily influenced by science.

So-called experts conflate questioning policy decisions with questioning data, methods, or discipline. Questioning policy, which is the subjective application of scientific findings, is immediately labeled as "anti-science" and thus is "anti-intellectual." Similarly, another strategy is to fund many scientific studies with the same collective outcomes, so even if people do try and question the scientific findings, the absolute volume and weight of these findings become nearly insurmountable—e.g., fifty-seven recent studies confirm a specific conclusion.

For example, if it starts with "studies suggest," "experts say," "scientists confirm," "according to research," "as indicated by the data," "professionals support," "polling data shows," "this society or association asserts," and so on, then it is unfortunately highly questionable. These strategies have led to a crisis in confidence because so many of these claims have failed or been refuted. There just seems to be so little interest in why or consequences for such abject failures—e.g., the recent COVID-19-related policies are a good example.

According to a recent study, respondents from 2022 showed little trust in government institutions, media, and large technology companies.[1] Respondents were provided with this prompt: "Now I am going to read you a list of institutions in American society. Please tell me how much confidence you, yourself, have in each one – a great deal, quite a lot, some or very little." The least trusted institutions (answering "a great deal" or "quite a lot") in order included Congress (7 percent), television news (11 percent), big business (14 percent), criminal justice system (14 percent), newspapers (16 percent), presidency (23 percent), supreme court (25 percent), large technology companies (26 percent), banks (27 percent), organized labor (28 percent), and public schools (28 percent). Every institution listed dropped significantly from the previous year.

This study also showed the lowest confidence ever recorded for the three branches of government. Five other institutions showed their lowest scores in over three decades. The only two institutions above fifty percent were the military (64 percent) and small businesses (68 percent). This lack of confidence and trust occurred across ages, demographics, and political affiliations. Americans' confidence in their core institutions has been lacking for most of the past fifteen years, but their trust in fundamental institutions has hit a new low in 2022. Most of the institutions are at historic lows; this data has been tracked since 1973.

These trends in trust are well-earned. A detailed review of all 2,047 biomedical and life-science research articles indexed by *PubMed* (as retracted on or before May 3, 2012) revealed that only 21.3 percent of retractions were attributable to error.[2] In contrast, 67.4 percent of retractions were attributable to misconduct, including fraud or suspected fraud (43.4 percent), duplicate publication (14.2 percent), and plagiarism (9.8 percent). Incomplete, uninformative, or misleading retraction announcements have led to a previous underestimation of the role of fraud in the ongoing retraction

1. Jones, "Confidence in US Institutions."
2. Fang et al., "Misconduct Accounts."

epidemic. The percentage of scientific articles retracted because of fraud has increased approximately ten-fold since 1975.

Some of the most retracted articles in recent history are associated with the COVID-19 pandemic.[3] The rush to produce findings and/or elevate professional status through publications compromised quality. The problem is that published studies, even of questionable value, can result in policy decisions. When those studies are retracted due to error or malfeasance, the policy is not questioned or modified. This is especially concerning when the funder of the studies benefits from the now debunked or compromised findings.

A 2003 study collected anonymous feedback from a large group of scientists, and the findings are especially troubling. John D. Greenwood and colleagues examined questionable research practices more directly. They conducted an online survey sent to nearly 6,000 researchers, including over 2,000 psychologists, to estimate the prevalence of the use of self-reported questionable research practices.[4]

What did they learn from the psychologists? One in ten respondents admitted to having falsified data, 67 percent reported they selectively reported results that "worked," 74 percent failed to report all their actual dependent variables, 71 percent reported that they continued to collect data until they achieved a significant result, 54 percent reported unexpected findings as having been hypothesized beforehand, and 58 percent excluded data to enhance the significance of their findings. The highest levels of self-admissions of questionable research practices were found among social psychologists (40 percent), followed by cognitive scientists (37 percent) and neuroscientists (35 percent). This is also concerning because behavioral science findings are now driving policy decisions, particularly around controversial topics like parenting, education, criminal justice, gender, diet, and equality.

Cumulatively and collectively, science is becoming a worldview—i.e., rationale empiricism, natural evolution, etc.—as people

3. Taros et al., "Retracted COVID-19 Articles."
4. Moreland, *The Disappearance*.

are told to follow and obey the science and to unite around the science for the collective or common good. Too often though that collective or common good seems like an erosion in freedom through tribalism, groupthink, group polarization, victim culture, and social contagions. It takes a lot of knowledge, courage, and resilience to fight against these cultural trends.

Be grateful if you see someone standing up to the authorities, especially if it comes at great risk, personally and professionally. It is the paradox of being trained to be innovative and forward-thinking but doing so within a system that encourages conformity and rewards entrenched hierarchy. This has led to many famous quotes about the nature of academia. In his *Notes on Nationalism*, George Orwell concludes, "One has to belong to the intelligentsia to believe things like that: no ordinary man could be such a fool."[5] While a bit less harsh yet capturing the same idea, British mathematician, philosopher, logician, and public intellectual Bertrand Russell stated, "We are faced with the paradoxical fact that education has become one of the chief obstacles to intelligence and freedom of thought."[6]

This ideal is exemplified by a quote from Martin Luther King, Jr.: "We must remember that intelligence is not enough. Intelligence plus character—that is the goal of true education. The complete education gives one not only power of concentration but worthy objectives upon which to concentrate."[7] Science specifically (and humankind more generally) cannot survive without science being restrained by moral authorities. Thus, Bonitto and Knox's book is a potent challenge to the status quo of the present anti-science movement.

Dr. Brian M. Kelley, PhD
Professor of Psychology
Liberty University

5. Orwell, *Notes on Nationalism*, 23.
6. Russell, *Conquest of Happiness*, 160.
7. Luther, "The Purpose of Education."

Preface

THIS BOOK WAS ORIGINALLY a thesis titled, *The Blind Scientist: A Critique of Neo-Darwinism's A Priori Assumptions*, which was a requirement for my Master of Arts in Christian Apologetics at Liberty University. Despite the thesis being a graduation requirement, I had other justifiable reasons for writing on this topic.

Currently, there are innumerable books on the market debating the heated subject of Evolution vs Religion (or Science vs Faith). As I am not a professional scientist, I did not set out to add any new scientific research on evolution or scientific methodology; however, as a reasonably skeptical student in the sciences, I noticed that many books (pro- or anti-evolutionism) fostered emotional factionalism between the opposing and corroborating sides, rather than striving to cultivate a neutral, balanced milieu for investigating scientific possibilities. This seemed quite unscientific to me and incongruous to the tenets of the scientific field.

Thus, I purposefully efforted to apply time-honored scientific methodology and objective, logical scrutiny in examining the concepts, contexts, and constructs surrounding postmodern scientism—not just to disprove the presuppositions and conclusions of neo-Darwinism—but to demonstrate that science, as of late, has become far too political, unempirically presumptuous, and precarious in its presentations of "the facts." Rather, this book seeks to carefully weigh the principles and practices of neo-Darwinian theory to determine which tenants could and should be considered truly *scientific* while practicing Jesus's teachings of *grace and truth*.

Science and the Christian faith must be based on objective, verifiable truths if they are to be any benefit to humanity. The importance of this topic is more than meets the eye, for two main reasons: 1) the social scope of the neo-Darwinian paradigm is gargantuan and 2) the potential cultural implications and applications of neo-Darwinism are chasmic.

Regarding point one, in the United States, most (if not all) public schools are instructed to teach neo-Darwinian evolutionary theory as a scientific fact. *The Next Generation Science Standards*, the framework introduced by the National Research Council in 2012, notes: "Science—and therefore science education—is central to the lives of all Americans, preparing them to be informed citizens in a democracy as knowledgeable consumers."[8]

Some twenty-six states utilize these new science standards in their high school curriculum. These states include the three largest school districts in the United States: New York City, Los Angeles Unified, and Chicago.[9] Additionally, the top ten most frequently used biology textbooks in high school utilizing these *Next Generation Standards* teach Darwinian evolution.[10] The result of this new approach is that neo-Darwinism has bled into academia's corners and cervices, suppressing healthy scientific thought in all communities of higher education. The toxicity of evolutionary psychology and social Darwinism (the application of neo-Darwinian theory) adds even more to the urgency of reconsidering neo-Darwinism's scientific fitness.

Regarding point two, the depth of neo-Darwinism's cultural reach has great reverberations with future youthful scientists. Neo-Darwinism, in its essence, makes the argument that intellectually

---

8. "HS-LS4-1 Biological Evolution."
9. US Census Bureau, "Top 10 Largest School Districts."
10. Ballen and Greene, "Walking and Talking," e2001630.

PREFACE

justifies atheism. Richard Dawkins once wrote, "Darwin made it possible to be an intellectually fulfilled atheist."[11] Without falling too deep into an exhaustive philosophical discussion (which will be covered in chapter six), if atheism is true and is genuinely acted out, one can justify a nihilistic, purposeless approach to life. If there is no purpose in living, then morality and ethics are irrelevant—a dark, dangerous sentiment when combined with scientific methodology, investigation, and applications (think Nazi Germany).

My goal for this modest book is to illuminate the importance of preconceived ideas when drawing intellectual inferences. One's presuppositions can heavily cloud how a thing is interpreted but true science has always been about filtering out personal biases. Potentially, by refusing to acknowledge the presuppositional "blinders" and "gaps" in their scientific methodology, some neo-Darwinian theorists may have unintentionlly created a scientific quagmire. Bad thinking leads to bad science, which inevitably ends in a bad society.

Yet, with so many competing views from educated, intelligent, and brilliant minds (from secular and religious researchers and thinkers), it is hoped that readers can comprehend that neo-Darwinism need not be the *only* intellectual postulation for the origin and mechanisms of life. Through a willingness to administer epistemic humility and intellectual honesty, it is possible to embrace an objective, productive approach that accurately demonstrates the honorable pursuits of scientific inquiry and investigation so needed in the world today.

---

11. Dawkins, *The Blind Watchmaker*, 6.

Acknowledgements

I WANT TO EXPRESS my deepest appreciation to my mother for her immense support. You have provided me with a place of shelter, peace, and love so that I can pursue my many endeavors. Not only that, but you have also been my spiritual support for all my life, and words cannot express the gratitude that I have for you in my heart. Thank you for being the best Mom a man could ask for in life.

To my best friend BJ, who has stuck with me through thick and thin. When the weight of the world is on my shoulders, you have always been there to help in many ways. Whether it is helping me proofread my papers, giving me ideas, or just listening to me for hours on the phone when I just need someone to talk to (even when you are working), you have always been there. Everyone needs a best friend like how Johnathan was to David. I am truly grateful that the Lord has put you in my life.

Dr. John Knox, thank you for your mentorship as my thesis supervisor, co-author of this book, and life mentor. You have not only refined me as a writer but also as a thinker, researcher, and man. This book would not have been a reality if it was not for you. You have exceeded all expectations. Every Joshua needs a Moses. Words cannot encapsulate my appreciation.

ACKNOWLEDGEMENTS

Dr. Gary Isaacs, thank you for your careful consideration as a reader of my thesis. Your critiques and suggestions have been refining and shaped me in more ways than you can imagine. Confering with a man of your intellectual caliber was an honor and a privilege.

Dr. Brian Kelley, thank you for carving out some time in your busy schedule to write the foreword to this book. Your expertise, wisdom, and contribution does not go unnoticed.

Lastly, and most importantly, I give all my gratitude, all my appreciation, and all my being to my Lord and Savior, Jesus Christ. You took the wretched man that I am and saved me, trained me, and guided me throughout my life's journey. Thank you for your patience with me and your enduring nature in preparing my heart for this book so that I may defend you with a humble heart.

1

The Relationship Between Science and Facts

"You cannot enter into an investigation with a philosophy that dictates the outcome."—J. Warner Wallace, *Cold-Case Christianity*

WHEN INVESTIGATING ANYTHING SCIENTIFICALLY—WHETHER it is a cold-case homicide, identifying office-work thievery, or determining the foundations of all life forms, it is quintessential to put aside all presuppositions to fairly ascertain the truth. If one's preconceived notions are unsupported by a lack of corroborating evidence (such as falsely accusing someone of murder or rape because of the complexion of their skin or presuming someone ate your lunch out of meanness), it may result in undesirable, even disastrous consequences for the parties involved. Even more so, if a group of scientists assumes that the origin of life can only come about via natural means because they reject the possibility of the existence of a higher deity (or life form), the scientists risk the integrity of the scientific endeavor, damaging the validity and reliability of their findings. These are common problems experienced historically and regularly wherein people assume something *a priori*.

In fact, many people *assume* something *prior* to the evidence as the result of their previous experience or presuppositions. These *a priori* assumptions often go unverified, which can be problematic; and yet, not all *a priori* assumptions are innately wrong. In fact, one can theoretically argue that no *a priori* assumptions are wrong, but only those that cannot withstand careful examination.

To illustrate, it is reasonable to assume (*a priori*) that all people are mortal, even if one never investigated every single person's death. One can make a deductive argument with the following syllogism:

1. All men are mortal.
2. Socrates is a man.
3. Therefore, Socrates is mortal.

The previous example illustrates deductive reasoning. Deductive reason occurs when the premises guarantee the truth of their conclusions.[1] Traditionally, all scientific, empirical facts are based on deductive theory (more on this in the next section). A scientific *theory*, however, is based on inductive theory, which occurs when the premises render a conclusion more *probable* than its competitors.[2]

This can be seen in the following example:

1. All the cars that I have seen in America have four wheels.
2. Therefore, every single car has four wheels.

Here, it is easy to see how assumptions play a more prominent role in the process of making inferences. One can quickly see that just because all cars in America have four wheels, it does not necessarily exclude the possibility of cars in other countries having three wheels (or five). Notice, however, that this does not mean that the argument is wrong, but rather that it lacks an exhaustive consideration since cars in other countries were not included while inferring the conclusion.

1. Moreland, *Philosophical Foundations*, 28.
2. Moreland, *Philosophical Foundations*, 28.

Respectively, this book will discuss what assumptions in the postmodern world of science can or cannot withstand careful examination.[3] Specifically, it will focus on the *a priori* assumptions that are necessary to arrive at neo-Darwinian conclusions (macro-evolution). This statement is quite charged. It can presuppose that 1) neo-Darwinism is not based solely on empirical data; 2) that assumptions shape the conclusions of neo-Darwinism; and 3) that there is debate on the veridicality of neo-Darwinism. This may sound like "scientific heresy" since the study of neo-Darwinism is a scientific theory that is considered a scientific fact among most scientists today. However, consequently, all of science relies on some form of assumptions. The question is, which ones are scientific?

1.1 Science and Assumptions

Science is derived from the Latin word, *Scientia*, which means "to know something." The modern name of science can appropriately mean the philosophy or study of nature. It entails observation, and it deals with that which can be tested via experiments.[4] However, there are other less conclusive ways to obtain scientific knowledge.[5] The category of science will dictate its level of dependency on assumptions based on its deductive or inductive nature. This can be loosely bifurcated into two types of sciences: quantitative and qualitative.

Quantitative science—hence its name—is quantifiable, meaning it can be measured and tested, mathematically. This secures much more reliability since mathematics is axiomatic, meaning self-evidently true. For example, one cannot prove that 2+2=4; it just is.

Sciences that fall into this quantitative category are chemistry and physics, although there are no absolutes. It is important

---

3. LaLand et al., "Evolutionary Theory."
4. Staddon, *Scientific Method*, 1.
5. Staddon, *Scientific Method*, 1.

to note that much of chemistry and physics is quantitative, but parts are also qualitative. However, for most of their studies, one can continually test these sciences and achieve the same results 100 percent of the time.

For example, the constant of gravity has always been tested to be 6.67×10^{-11} Newtons kg^{-2} m^2, or the boiling point of water at normal atmospheric pressure has always been 100° Celsius/212° Fahrenheit. These laws of nature must be assumed *a priori* when conducting experiments. The chemist does not test and retest the water's boiling point to ensure it does not change when conducting an experiment. Furthermore, physicists assume *a priori* that mathematics works all the time when doing their calculations. However, since mathematics can be empirically verified, the real *a priori* assumption here is that *truth remains true all the time.*

Qualitative sciences are less quantifiable. These are biology and the social sciences like psychology, sociology, and even history. Like its name (qualitative), these rely on qualities. However, even though biology and the social sciences would be considered qualitative science, many parts of these sciences are quantifiable.

For the most part, however, the qualities these sciences rely on can be derived from concepts, appearances, experiences, and symbols. For example, a case study for determining which exercise produces the best results for jumping ability would be qualitative in nature while using quantitative features like the measurement of gravity to test the results. However, the conclusions derived from the results are based on the concepts and correlations found from the study. This creates more nuance than a mathematical calculation. This, by nature, makes qualitative studies rely more on philosophical principles to interpret the data, which is completely appropriate and scientific. So, not all *a priori* assumptions are bad. They are necessary to do science. The question now comes, what *a priori* assumptions are bad?

One can encapsulate this by understanding falsifiability—having the ability to be proven false. The reality is that most things cannot be proven within 100 percent of certainty. For example, the laws of nature cannot be proved within 100 percent of certainty but are identified and formulated through diligent observation.[6] The constant of gravity has never been proved, because it is just as unprovable as all other laws of nature. It is assumed to be universally valid because it has been shown to be true in millions of experiences within reality.[7] Therefore, a theorem must be formulated in such a way that it can be proven false.[8]

For example, the law of gravity could easily be refuted if things started to float randomly and irregularly in the air. With this scenario, hypotheses come into play. Hypotheses are assumptions based on the facts established by these theorems (laws of nature). If any part of that hypothesis contradicts known theorems, then the hypothesis should be rejected.[9] This is where something called a paradigm is formulated. A paradigm can be perceived when a system of these hypotheses pervade an entire scientific era.[10] Yet, if this paradigm has been derived based on assumptions strictly dictated by a specific worldview or faith commitment, it creates difficulty in reconciling it with objectivity.[11]

The scientific paradigm of geo-centricity that Copernicus refuted is a great example of this notion.[12] The geocentric model provided great explanatory power for what Aristotle observed in addition to his worldview;[13] he supposed the gods created the heavenly bodies and mankind. This makes sense, according to ancient Greek philosophy, because the gods created Earth and would, therefore, make everything revolve around its habitable creation.

In that case, it would explain why Aristotle concluded with the geocentric model based on his observations of the sun and planets appearing to revolve around the Earth. This short

6. Gitt, *In the Beginning*, 27.
7. Gitt, *In the Beginning*, 27.
8. Gitt, *In the Beginning*, 31.
9. Gitt, *In the Beginning*, 23.
10. Gitt, *In the Beginning*, 23.
11. Gitt, *In the Beginning*, 23.
12. Gitt, *In the Beginning*, 23–24.
13. This example of Copernicus and geo-centricity will be further elaborated on in section 6.2, "Copernicus and a Scientific Revolution."

example demonstrates how one's worldview can shape personal assumptions used to ascertain scientific conclusions—even those integrating science and faith.

1.2 The Relationship Between Science and Faith

Everyone has a worldview. Whether it is Christianity, Judaism, Islam, Hinduism, Buddhism, Agnosticism, or Atheism—everyone has a lens of reality through which they view the world. Each worldview provides its own answer to the big questions in life: Who am I? Why am I here? How did I get here? Moreover, all worldviews are based on faith. The theist has faith in God, the polytheist has faith in the gods, the pantheist has faith that a divine spirit is in everything, the agnostic has faith in the unknowable, and the atheist has faith solely in empirical nature and physics. This is because all people espouse beliefs in something that they trust, providing meaning and direction in how and why they live their lives.

Faith is not simply a thoughtless blind belief in something which is not seen; it is an action taken on the evidence one derives from her surroundings. For example, if one sees a chair and says he believes it will hold him up, his faith is not revealed until the person takes action to sit in the chair. Coincidentally, the evidence that the chair looked sturdy, and the *a priori* assumption that most chairs do not collapse on impact, facilitated the person's trust in sitting in the chair. This parallels science because even science relies on faith. In John Staddon's *Scientific Method: How Science Works, Fails to Work, and Pretends to Work*, he states, "Faith in the invariance of natural laws is essential to science. But it is faith, just like belief in transubstantiation or the afterlife."[14]

As previously mentioned, even the laws of nature cannot be proven within 100 percent of certainty. Therefore, scientists must have faith that the laws of nature will not change in the future and have not changed in the past. This is called the Principle of

---

14. Staddon, *Scientific Method*, 28.

Uniformity.[15] Scientists then must work out this faith by trusting in this principle to do science. Often, there is immense empirical evidence for scientific conclusions, and equating those empirical findings to the same hierarchal level of faith as believing in the afterlife would be incongruent.

Instead, the question this book answers is whether there are unscientific and faith-based presuppositions generated through an atheistic lens that are used to support the assumptions necessary for neo-Darwinian conclusions. If there are, it reveals that neo-Darwinism is not as scientific as the world thinks (or is as promoted to be). Before diving into this, however, a brief history of what is called neo-Darwinism must be considered.

1.3 A Brief History: Darwinism to Neo-Darwinism

Charles Darwin and Alfred Wallace would be considered the major contributors to the theory known as Darwinism. In fact, it was Alfred Wallace who came up with the well-known term today, "Natural Selection." In 1859, Charles Darwin published his first book on evolutionary biology named, *On the Origin of Species*, which revolutionized the world of science. In his book, Darwin argued for more of a compound theory with many sub-theories, but nonetheless, it made the case that all life has descended from one ancient but unseen parent and, consequently, has inherited something in common by way of natural selection.[16]

Interestingly, Alfred Wallace—although he had a significant contribution to this theory— eventually denounced the theory of evolution via natural selection. Wallace stated,

> There are certain purely physical characteristics of the human race which are not explicable on the theory of variation and survival of the fittest. The brain, the organs

---

15. Geisler and Turek, *Don't Have Enough Faith*, 177.
16. Darwin, *On the Origin*, 384.

of speech, the hand, and the external form of man, offer some special difficulties in this respect.[17]

What seems to be the issue here was that there needed to be more evidence to consider whether key Darwinian conclusions were valid or even plausible. It seemed (according to Wallace) that certain things were presupposed to be true to guarantee the outcome(s) of Darwinian theory. Additionally, shortly after the publication of *On the Origin of the Species*, Harvard geologist and paleontologist Louis Agassiz pointed out that the sudden appearance and disappearance of unrelated different species shown in the fossil record did not support Darwin's claims.[18]

In defense of Agassiz's criticism, Darwin wrote,

> If my theory be true, it is indisputable that before the lowest Silurian [Cambrian]stratum was deposited, long periods elapsed, as long as, or probably far longer than, the whole interval from the Silurian age to the present day; and that during these vast, *yet quite unknown* [emphasis mine], periods of time, the world swarmed with living creatures. To the question why we do not find records of these vast primordial periods, I can give no satisfactory answer.[19]

This suggests that if numerous species came to life all at once instead of a process of gradual evolution—from simple to complex and from a single common ancestor—then, by Darwin's standard, it would contradict his original theory. However, unlike today, Darwin and Alfred did not have the knowledge of genetics, which is crucial for the neo-Darwinian paradigm. One could argue that the evidence of the fossil record could not, on its own, refute the synchronic Darwinian model.

Seven years after Darwin's *Origin of Species*, German monk and geneticist Gregor Mendel proposed a theory that genetic

---

17. Wallace, "Sir Charles Lyell," 391.
18. Davis, "How Darwin Failed."
19. Darwin, *On the Origin*, 286.

material is transmitted as units, known today as Mendelian genetics.[20] Mendel's research remained obscure for about three decades where its "rediscovery" challenged the acceptance of Darwinism. Russian-born American naturalist and experimental geneticist Theodosius Dobzhansky synthesized these Mendelian genetics with Darwinian evolution. This is where science gets the term, *Modern Evolutionary Synthesis* (a.k.a., "neo-Darwinism").

Unlike original Darwinism, here, selection is introduced after heredity.[21] This does not mean that selection is less important as a mechanism, but it has a different logical position in neo-Darwinian theory.[22] Today, neo-Darwinism can be defined as "life evolving to its present state of complexity and diversity via a purposeless material mechanism of random genetic change and natural selection."[23]

There are four assumptions within this one statement:

1. Life evolved.
2. This evolution is purposeless.
3. The process uses random genetic changes.
4. The process uses natural selection as a mechanism for only promoting more offspring.

Here, God is unnecessary for this process to operate, but a theistic evolutionist like Francis Collins or Alister McGrath would still be considered "neo-Darwinian" in that they believe that God directs the evolutionary process. Consequently (and ironically), since the origin of life is a type of forensic science and cannot be tested in a lab, theoretically, only God would know how it all happened. However, one could ask, if neo-Darwinism provides an adequate explanation for the naturalistic origin and mechanisms of life, what must be true in support of its conclusions?

---

20. Miko, 134.
21. Ruse, *Charles Darwin*, 87.
22. Ruse, *Charles Darwin*, 87.
23. Johnson, "Introduction," 1–3.

1.4 Neo-Darwinism and Its Assumptions

Five concepts must be true for neo-Darwinism to be true. These include gradualism, the tree of life hypothesis, the evidence of micro-evolutionary change accounting for macro-evolutionary change, time and chance, and methodological naturalism.

Gradualism is the notion that all life has evolved via a long process of small and minute steps in the direction of simple to more complex. The tree of life hypothesis hypothesizes that all life came from a single-parent organism and that lineage can be traced via an interconnected tree of life. The micro-evolutionary to macro-evolutionary assumption is that the empirical evidence we observe within species—adaptability and change over time—can further correlate to the transitioning of species—from sea creatures to land animals. The time and chance assumption simply assumes that with enough time, there is a plausible chance that genetic mutations can account for the complexity of functioning organisms we know today. Lastly, methodological naturalism is the notion that all scientific theories *must* explain any and all phenomena via material causes.

Prima facie, these *a priori* assumptions seem to have tremendous explanatory power. They provide the "Ah, that explains why we observe this" moment—especially in Darwin's findings with the finches on the Galapagos islands. Yet, when looking at the corroborating evidence for these five concepts, it appears that all five are unsupported, unconvincing, and seem to be held onto due to individual/emotional biases.

If this is true, then it creates immense problems for the pontification of neo-Darwinism as an intractable fact. What will be discovered in this book aligns with the introductory quotation of J. Warner Wallace: "You simply cannot enter into an investigation with a philosophy that dictates the outcome,"[24] concluding that all five of these concepts seem to be used to dictate the outcome of neo-Darwinism rather than letting the evidence speak for itself.

---

24. Wallace, *Cold Case Christianity*, 30.

Somewhat unsurprisingly, the tenuous *a priori* assumptions for neo-Darwinism have created a schism in the world of science and philosophy. Therefore, a review of this dilemma will be discussed in the next chapter.

2

A Summary of Neo-Darwinian Scholarship

THE FOLLOWING LITERATURE REVIEW, while not exhaustive, explores the different schools of thought within the professional scientific and philosophical world regarding neo-Darwinism, scientific theory, and the *a priori* assumptions needed to arrive at neo-Darwinian conclusions. This chapter will be divided up into four sections. The first will focus on Christian scholars who disagree with an atheistic postulation of neo-Darwinism. Theistic evolutionists will be included in this section since this chapter emphasizes how different worldviews can affect how one interprets raw data. The second concerns non-Christian scholars who disagree with neo-Darwinism; the third includes non-Christian scholars who see some problems with neo-Darwinism, and the fourth centers on non-Christian scholars who strongly hold to neo-Darwinism.

2.1 Christian Scholars Who Disagree with Neo-Darwinism

John Lennox, mathematician and bioethicist Emeritus Professor at Oxford University, believes that the nature of science makes it hard to consider most scientific theories as intractable facts (see Figure 1). Lennox is convinced that there is no one scientific method that is completely agreed upon in the scientific community.[1] This is due to the nature of science, itself.

Lennox believes that different fields in the sciences carry more authority than others. He writes, "Scientific theory that is based on repeated observation and experimentation is likely to, and should, carry more authority than that which is not."[2] He believes that scientific theories should be abandoned if the facts defy every rational explanation.[3] The problem that Lennox sees within the scientific community is an inappropriate equivocation of "rational explanation" and "natural explanation."[4] He calls this, "At best an indicator of a strong prejudice, at worst a category mistake."[5]

This is where he rejects neo-Darwinism because it holds to an *a priori assumption* called methodological naturalism, which is the ground rule of modern science—where scientists seek explanations based on natural causes alone. Lennox concludes this to be unscientific and rather more of a philosophical discourse or even a faith commitment.

This is demonstrated in a remark by evolutionary biologist Richard Lewontin:

> It is not that the methods and institutions of science somehow compel us to accept a material explanation of the phenomenal world, but, on the contrary, that we are forced by our *a priori* adherence to material causes to create an apparatus of investigation and a set of concepts that produce material explanations, no matter how counter-intuitive, no matter how mystifying to the

---

1. Lennox, *God's Undertaker*, 39.
2. Lennox, *God's Undertaker*, 39.
3. Lennox, *God's Undertaker*, 34.
4. Lennox, *God's Undertaker*, 34.
5. Lennox, *God's Undertaker*, 34.

uninitiated. Moreover, that materialism is absolute, for we cannot allow a Divine Foot in the door.[6]

Lennox adds, "It is a tautology to say that 'materialists cannot allow a Divine foot in the door.' Materialism rejects both the Divine foot and, come to think of it, the door as well."[7] Lennox notices that there is evidence that gives a better reason to postulate the non-material rather than the material, itself. The primary evidence in his book, *God's Undertaker*, is that the cause of information—precisely in DNA—is better explained by a mind rather than material causes. For many, whenever one sees information, one always postulates a mind behind the message; therefore, Lennox concludes that it is plausible to conclude that the message of DNA is from a mind rather than a natural, random, mindless process.

Stephen Meyer, a philosopher of science and a former geophysicist, would consider Lennox's assertions to be correct. Like Lennox, he believes that there is no defensible definition of neo-Darwinian science.[8] Meyer distinguishes the authoritative differences based on the inductive nature of some sciences. He believes that there is a coherent distinction between historical and non-historical science.[9]

In addition, Meyer rejects methodological naturalism because it is not within the scientific frame of its science category. In the context of neo-Darwinism and the origin of life, he writes, "The historical question about biological origins is not 'Which materialistic scenario will prove adequate?' but 'How did life as we know it actually arise on earth?'"[10] Meyer believes that the answer to this question can be argued based on evidence of the Cambrian period's fossil record.

In *Darwin's Doubt*, Meyer explains that the missing fossils in the Precambrian era and the explosion of new life forms

6. Lewontin, "Billions and Billions."
7. Lennox, *God's Undertaker*, 36.
8. Meyer, *Darwin's Doubt*, 309.
9. Meyer, "Laws, Causes, and Facts," 32.
10. Meyer, "Laws, Causes, and Facts," 34.

in the Cambrian era discovered in the Burgess Shale create great problems for the neo-Darwinian *a priori* assumptions of gradualism. Meyer writes, "The problem posed by the Burgess Shale is not the increase in complexity, but the sudden quantum leap in complexity."[11] Meyer finds this to be a problem for neo-Darwinian conclusions because one of the main assumptions for Darwinism was a gradual mechanism of evolution. He argues that the findings in the Burgess Shale (as evidence for the "explosion" of new life forms) pose a problem for the hypothesis of gradualism.

In addition, like Lennox, Meyer talks about the problem with DNA. He gives a scientific and mathematical explanation for the improbability of DNA mutating via a random, unguided, and mindless process. Meyer utilized molecular biologist Douglas Axe's estimation that the classical model of gene evolution is about 10^{77}.[12] He argues, "The classical model of gene evolution, random mutations must thrash about aimlessly in immense combinatorial space, a space that could not be explored by this means in the entire history of life on earth, let alone in the few million years of the Cambrian explosion."[13] Meyer seems to be suggesting that chance and time are not enough for neo-Darwinian conclusions to be valid.

In correlation to chance, mathematician and philosopher William Dembski makes an argument against inferring scientific facts based on chance. In Dembski's *The Design Inference,* he argues that inferring design can be a more logical method of inference than chance when it comes to a mystery about something since design inferences are used to elicit insight to solve the mystery.[14] Dembski argues that many scenarios used the design inference. Patent offices, copyright offices, insurance companies, actuarial firms, statistical consultants, cryptographers, forensic scientists, and detectives all use design inference and are considered logical.[15]

---

11. Meyer, *Darwin's Doubt*, 36.
12. Meyer, *Darwin's Doubt*, 203.
13. Meyer, *Darwin's Doubt*, 203.
14. Dembski, *Design Inference*, 24.
15. Dembski, *Design Inference*, 22.

The design inference can be defined as eliminating the regularity of chance to limit explanatory options. It has to do with events conforming to patterns; however, "It does not entail a causal story, much less an intelligent agent."[16] However, Dembski notes that routinely, the reason an event conforms to a pattern is that an intelligent agent arranged it so.[17] The design inference's main importance is detecting and measuring information.[18] Like Lennox and Meyer, Dembski considers the nature of the information to be logically inferred via Intelligent Design.

Utilizing the mathematical model, Cornell University geneticist John C. Sanford argues that more time and more chance would elicit more genetic extinction rather than less. His coined term, "genetic entropy," proposes that "mutational entropy appears to be so strong within large genomes that selection cannot reverse it. This makes eventual extinction of such genomes inevitable."[19]

Engineer Werner Gitt concurs with Lennox, Meyer, and Dembski about the postulation of information plausibly coming from a mind. In his book, *In the Beginning Was Information*, Gitt argues that information always postulates a mind behind the message. He argues that when scientists look at the five levels of information: statistics, syntax, semantics, pragmatics, and apobetics, they can know which levels of information contain a message caused by a mind. He argues that when as one looks at DNA, it contains the most complex level of information—which are pragmatics and apobetics.

With this, Gitt suggests that information is not material but needs a material medium. He says that information is not life, but the information in cells is essential for all living beings.[20] Therefore, information is a necessary prerequisite for life, and life is, therefore, nonmaterial.[21] However, life is not information

16. Dembski, *Design Inference*, 226.
17. Dembski, *Design Inference*, 227.
18. Dembski, *Design Inference*, 228.
19. Sanford, *Genetic Entropy*, 144.
20. Gitt, *In the Beginning*, 81.
21. Gitt, *In the Beginning*, 81.

but matter and information are essential for life.[22] Gitt writes, "Information requires matter for storage and transmission, life requires information, biological life requires matter as a necessary medium, and information and matter fall far short in describing life, but life depends on the necessary conditions prevailing at the lower levels."[23] With this, he concludes, "The information present in living organisms requires an intelligent source. Man could not have been this source, so that the only remaining possibility is that there must have been a Creator."[24]

Francis Collins, the former leader of the International Human Genome Project and director of the National Institutes of Health, is a theistic evolutionist who believes that a faith in God can be a rational choice and that the principles of faith are complementary with the principles of science.[25] In his view, there is no conflict between being a rigorous scientist and a person who believes in a God who takes a personal interest in our lives.[26] Moreover, he believes that there is molecular evidence that supports the theory of evolution.[27] Namely, the existence of repetitive "junk DNA" in shared locations along the DNA of humans and mice.[28]

To elaborate, humans and mice contain these things called Ancient Repetitive Elements (AREs) of common ancestors. These are elements that arise from "jumping" genes that are capable of copying and inserting themselves in various locations in the genome, usually without functional consequences (junk DNA).[29] There have been discoveries of precisely truncated AREs in the same place in humans and mice genomes. This means that a scientist can identify a decapitated and defunct ARE in a parallel position in the human and mouse genome. This correlation, in

22. Gitt, *In the Beginning*, 81.
23. Gitt, *In the Beginning*, 82.
24. Gitt, *In the Beginning*, 97–98.
25. Collins, *Language of God*, 3.
26. Collins, *Language of God*, 6.
27. Collins, *Language of God*, 141.
28. Collins, *Language of God*, 173.
29. Collins, *Language of God*, 135.

Collin's opinion, is compelling evidence that this insertion event of AREs must have occurred in an ancestor that was common to both the human and the mouse.[30]

Additionally, the correlation of chromosome patterning in chimpanzees and humans is compelling evidence for the mechanism of evolution. Collins notes that the difference in the chromosome number between humans and chimpanzees (twenty-three pairs for humans, twenty-four for chimpanzees) appears to be a consequence of the second ancestral chromosome fusing together to generate our human chromosome two.[31] With this, there is a special sequence that occurs at the tips of all primate chromosomes that do not occur anywhere else. Interestingly enough, that same special sequence found in chimpanzees is also found in the middle of a human's second fused chromosome, which is exactly where it would be predicted within the evolutionary model of genetics.[32]

All this evidence points in favor to the neo-Darwinian paradigm; however, unlike the neo-Darwinian position, Collins admits that science has not answered the question of how a self-replicating organism arose in the first place.[33] As he once stated, "We simply do not know."[34] In contrast to atheist evolutionary biologist Richard Dawkins, Collins says:

> Dawkin's argument that evolution fully accounts for biological complexity and the origins of humankind, so there is no more need for God, rightly relieves God of the responsibility for multiple acts of special creation for each species on the planet, but it does not disprove the idea that God worked out His creative plan by means of evolution.[35]

Alister McGrath is another theistic evolutionist who draws a dichotomy between Darwinism as a science and Darwinism

---

30. Collins, *Language of God*, 135.
31. Collins, *Language of God*, 135.
32. Collins, *Language of God*, 135.
33. Collins, *Language of God*, 90.
34. Collins, *Language of God*, 90.
35. Collins, *Language of God*, 163–64.

as an ideology. He notes that the main variable factor influencing Darwinian theory has to do with its openness to falsification. Thus, he believes Darwinism contains an ideology beyond scientific investigation because it is a creedal statement, not a scientific viewpoint. He says, "Ideologies are reinforced by social structures, which frequently use power as a means of reinforcing the regnant ideology and can be seen in the public school system, academic culture, and the media which we see today."[36]

On page one of McGrath's *Darwinism and the Divine*, he notes that the nature of science itself cannot answer every question but can raise questions that go beyond the realm of science.[37] He also talks about the nature of faith and science and how it deals with *a priori* assumptions demanded by the application of the scientific method.[38] McGrath concurs with Lennox, Meyer, and Gitt in that all science embraces certain *a priori* assumptions, but the importance is whether these assumptions are scientific. This is where McGrath seems to press on methodological naturalism being one of these unscientific assumptions because it is not always the empirical outcome.

Like John Lennox, McGrath comments on Richard Lewontin's comment on holding onto materialism and not allowing a divine foot in the door. McGrath says that this comment excluded God because of a prior dogmatic commitment to materialism—not on account of a commitment to the investigation of nature, wherever this leads us. He writes, "Materialism is here regarded as the controlling and foreclosing presupposition, not the warranted empirical outcome, of the scientific method."[39]

Within the context of methodological naturalism, philosopher Alvin Plantinga believes that science should be objective, public, sharable, publicly verifiable, and equally available to everyone regardless of their religious or metaphysical proclivities.[40]

36. McGrath, *Darwinism and the Divine*, 36.
37. McGrath, *Darwinism and the Divine*, 1.
38. McGrath, *Darwinism and the Divine*, 33.
39. McGrath, *Darwinism and the Divine*, 33.
40. Plantinga, "Methodological Naturalism," 144.

However, Plantinga thinks that it is absurd to claim neutrality in all science based on the inductive nature of some sciences. He thinks that certain things (like the Pythagorean theorem) are religiously neutral.[41] Plantinga also thinks that methodological naturalism should be rejected when he writes that there is "little to be said for it, when examined coolly in the light of day, the arguments for it seem weak indeed."[42]

Norman Geisler and Frank Turek are Christian apologists who note the problem of the origin of life and neo-Darwinian conclusions. They define science as a search for causes.[43] They assert that the nature of the science of the origin of life is in a completely different category from normal, empirical sciences. Similar to Meyer, they write, "The origin of life is a forensic question that requires us to piece together evidence much like [how] detectives piece together evidence from a murder."[44]

Also, like McGrath, they note that philosophical suppositions are used when searching for causes and (therefore) cannot be the result of them. The big assumption that Geisler and Turek claim scientists commit to is the *a priori* assumption of logic. They believe that scientists assume—by faith—that reason and the scientific method allow scientists to accurately understand the world that people observe. They assert, "You can't prove the tools of science—the laws of logic, the Law of Causality, the Principle of Uniformity, or the reliability of observation—by running some kind of experiment."[45] This presumption is appropriate to them because it is in line with common sense and with the evidential, observation reality that confirms,

> Data is always interpreted by scientists. When those scientists let their personal preferences or unproven philosophical assumptions dictate their interpretation of evidence, they do exactly what they accuse religious

41. Plantinga, "Methodological Naturalism," 143.
42. Plantinga, "Methodological Naturalism," 154.
43. Geisler and Turek, *Don't Have Enough Faith*, 120.
44. Geisler and Turek, *Don't Have Enough Faith*, 117.
45. Geisler and Turek, *Don't Have Enough Faith*, 127–28.

people of doing, they let their ideology dictate their conclusions. When that's the case, their conclusions should be questioned, because they may not be nothing more than philosophical presuppositions passed off as scientific fact.[46]

In examining the presuppositions of materialist scientists, Geisler and Turek point out that they seem to ignore the irreducible complexity observed within nature. They hold strongly to biochemist Michael Behe's argument for irreducible complexity.

Michael Behe responds to Darwinian assumptions about irreducibly complex systems in his book, *Darwin's Black Box*. Behe places major emphasis on defining irreducible complexity. He defines it as a "single system composed of several well-matched, interacting parts that contribute to the basic function, wherein the removal of any one of the parts causes the system to effectively cease functioning."[47] Because of this, he argues that an irreducibly complex system cannot be made by slight successive modifications because any precursor to an irreducibly complex system that is a missing part will be non-functional.[48] This challenges the assumption of gradualism. Behe's main finding focuses on the bacterial flagellum, which he argues is an irreducibly complex system and thus posits the need for an Intelligent Intercessor.

Still, Francis Collins disagrees with Behe with the claim that research has fundamentally "undercut" this position of irreducible complexity.[49] Regardless, Behe also addresses the plausibility of random mutations generating animals and argues that because of irreducible complexity, mutations cannot change the instructions in one single step.[50] His famous example was the mousetrap. He argues that if you have a five-part mousetrap, and when one part of the mouse trap is missing, the whole contraption will not

---

46. Geisler and Turek, *Don't Have Enough Faith*, 128.
47. Behe, *Darwin's Black Box*, 42.
48. Behe, *Darwin's Black Box*, 42–43.
49. Collins, *Language of God*, 192.
50. Behe, *Darwin's Black Box*, 44.

work anymore. Ken Miller disagreed with Behe's point and built a mousetrap with four parts on a televised debate on PBS.

Behe responded that it only elicits the need for intelligence and in addition, substituting "the four parts" does not negate the claim. He argued that if one takes the mouse board out and uses the floor, he is still using the floor as a board. This received major criticism from skeptics, but Behe replied, "If one removes a part of a clearly defined, irreducibly complex system, the system itself immediately and necessarily ceases to function."[51]

Christian Scholars Who Disagree with Neo-Darwinism		
Name	Worldview	Rationale
John Lennox	Intelligent Design	Information in DNA better explains an immaterial mind to be the cause of life rather than a material cause.
Stephen Myer	Intelligent Design	The abrupt arrival of new and complex life forms in the Cambrian period creates problems for gradualism.
William Dembski	Intelligent Design	Inferences to design and intelligent agency are better explanatory options than an inference to chance.
John Sanford	Intelligent Design	With more time and chance, genetic entropy would elicit more genetic extinction than function.
Werner Gitt	Creationism	It has always been observed that information comes from an immaterial mind.
Francis Collins	Theistic Evolution	Chromosomal correlation patterns among chimps and humans posit good evidence for an evolutionary process but it is not sufficient to explain how life first started.
Alister McGrath	Theistic Evolution	Neo-Darwinism adopts a creedal statement of methodological naturalism, which seems unscientific.
Alvin Plantinga	Intelligent Design	The inductive nature of science should enable one to understand that methodological naturalism is not exhaustive.
Norman Geisler	Intelligent Design	The tools needed to do science (logic, causality, uniformity, reliable observation) presuppose agency rather than mindlessness.
Frank Turek	Intelligent Design	Similar to Geisler, the tools needed to do science (logic, causality, uniformity, reliable observation) presuppose agency rather than mindlessness.
Michael Behe	Intelligent Design	Irreducibly complex systems create issues for a gradual evolutionary process.

Figure 1 © Alexander J. Bonitto, 2023

2.2 Non-Christian Scholars Who Disagree with Neo-Darwinism.

Mathematician and philosopher David Berlinski is a secular Jew who has written much about neo-Darwinian dogma (see Figure 2). In his books, *The Devil's Delusion* and *The Deniable Darwin*, Berlinski writes a polemic against the ideology of neo-Darwinism and how he finds its dogma to be unsupported and tyrannical. One of Berlinski's main issues is that the neo-Darwinian paradigm is considered an unassailable fact. Berlinski writes, "If no theory is right, how can 'the idea that human minds are the

---

51. Behe, "Reply to My Critics," 693.

A SUMMARY OF NEO-DARWINIAN SCHOLARSHIP

product of evolution' be 'unassailable fact?' If this idea is not an unassailable fact, why must we put aside the idea that man was created in the image of God?"[52]

Another big issue Berlinski sees is that the world of science is trying to disprove the existence of God. Yet, he argues that this is not a scientific claim. He thinks that to put aside the idea that people are created in the image of God, then the opposing reason should be a better reason. Berlinski writes, "If they are no good, why champion them? And they are no good. So why champion them?"[53]

Berlinksi also argues against the probability for self-replication for the origin of life. Berlinski notes[54] that the odds of one single molecule self-replication would be 10^{60}. With this number, Berlinski writes against the mental strong-holds that he claims neo-Darwinists fanatically claim, by saying, "No betting man would take them, no matter how attractive the payoff, and neither presumably would nature."[55]

Another way Berlinski formulates his polemic against materialism is by explaining the complexity of the human eye, the human mind, and aesthetics. He writes about the process of how light hits the eye in the form of photons and goes through a whole process that gives people sight. With this phenomenon of sight, people perceive something called beauty. He writes, "How do the twitching nerves, chemical exchanges, electrical flashes, and computational routines of the human eye and brain provide a human being with his experiences."[56]

Only somewhat similar to Berlinski, Thomas Nagel—Emeritus Professor of Philosophy and Law at New York University—is an atheist who rejects the neo-Darwinian paradigm. He expresses that he lacks the *sensus divinitatis* that compels people to believe in God and does not invoke a transcendent being with his denial of

---

52. Berlinski, *Devil's Delusion*, 178.
53. Berlinski, *Devil's Delusion*, 165.
54. Berlinski and Klinghoffer, *Deniable Darwin*, 284.
55. Berlinski and Klinghoffer, *Deniable Darwin*, 284.
56. Berlinski, *Devil's Delusion*, 204.

neo-Darwinism but intends to highlight the complications to the "immanent character of the natural order."[57] In addition, he disagrees with the Intelligent Design argument that the only alternative is a reductionist theory that people like Richard Dawkins hold. Yet, unlike Richard Dawkins, who believes that Darwinism makes it possible to be an intellectually fulfilled atheist,[58] Nagel thinks there are massive problems with neo-Darwinism.

He writes in the context of neo-Darwinism, "It seems to me that, as it is usually presented, the current orthodoxy about the cosmic order is the product of governing assumptions that are unsupported, and that it flies in the face of common sense."[59] Nagel also thinks that natural selection is an inadequate explanation for the mechanism of mutational change. He also thinks that neo-Darwinism is an "assumption governing the scientific project rather than a well-confirmed scientific hypothesis."[60] Furthermore, Nagel suggests that the dogmatic view of neo-Darwinism is absurd.

He believes it is wrong to call Intelligence Designists (like Michael Behe, Stephen Meyer, and David Berlinski) "stupid." He writes, "Even if one is not drawn to the alternative of an explanation by the actions of a designer, the problems that these iconoclasts pose for the orthodox scientific consensus should be taken seriously. They do not deserve the scorn with which they are commonly met. It is manifestly unfair."[61]

57. Nagel, *Mind and Cosmos*, 11.
58. Dawkins, *Blind Watchmaker*, 71.
59. Nagel, *Mind and Cosmos*, 5.
60. Nagel, *Mind and Cosmos*, 11.
61. Nagel, *Mind and Cosmos*, 10.

Non-Christian Scholars Who Disagree with Neo-Darwinism		
Name	Worldview	Rationale
David Berlinski	Secular Judaism	Aesthetic phenomenon like beauty seems to contradict a strict materialistic worldview.
Thomas Nagel	Atheism	Natural selection is an inadequate explanation for mutational change.

Non-Christian Scholars That Observe Problems with Neo-Darwinism		
Name	Worldview	Rationale
Christian Schwabe	Complex Evolution	The study of chemistry suggests a "lawn" of life rather than a "tree" of life.
Gerd Müller	Non-Theist?	Morphological issues create problems for evolutionary theory beyond the realm of genetics.
Stuart Newman	Non-Theist?	Similar to Müller, Morphological issues create problems for evolutionary theory beyond the realm of genetics.
Simon Morris	Leans Towards Theistic Evolution	The burst of complex life forms in the Cambrian period undermines gradualism.
Pat Willmer	Non-Theist?	Genomic changes among species invalidate traditional "tree of life" classifications.

Figure 2 © Alexander J. Bonitto, 2023

2.3 Non-Christian Scholars That Observe Problems with Neo-Darwinism

Christian Schwabe was a biochemist at Harvard who believes that due to the nature of the neo-Darwinian paradigm (see Figure 2), making hypotheses cannot be proved within 100 percent of certainty. He asserted that a current hypothesis can be disproved when the evidence drives beyond the foundation of the prior hypothesis. In the beginning of his book, *The Genomic Potential Hypothesis*, Schwabe argues against the tree of life hypothesis based on the fossil record of the Cambrian period in addition to the nature of chemistry. Schwabe suggests that if life came from chemicals, it would result in a "lawn" of life rather than a "tree" of life. He even thinks that the "tree of life" hypothesis is not scientific. He writes, "To invoke strings of beneficial mutations that suffice to reshape one animal into the shape of another is not merely unreasonable, it is not science."[62]

In 2003's *Origination of Organismal Form*, scientists Gerd Müller and Stuart Newman include a chapter named, "Problems of Morphological Evolution," which illuminates the morphological issues with the neo-Darwinian paradigm. In this section, the scientists talk about the same evidence of the Burgess Shale that Stephen Meyer spoke about in his book, *Darwin's Doubt*.

62. Schwabe, *Genomic Potential Hypothesis*, 1.

All of them saw problems with the current neo-Darwinian paradigm. Simon Conway Morris noticed the "stunning burst of metazoan forms at the beginning of the Cambrian."[63] Morris believes that if Darwin returned today, his suspicion, "articulated in chapter 9 of *On the Origin of Species*, that the seemingly abrupt appearance of skeletons near the beginning of the Cambrian might undermine his notion of evolution proceeding by slow and steady change" could be laid to rest.[64]

Pat Willmer noticed the "Recurrence of similar design solutions in different phylogenetic lineages, despite their absence in a common ancestor."[65] In her chapter, she observed that there are many sources of change in the genome that may invalidate traditional assumptions about homology and the independence of characters.[66] Gerd Müller proposed that the "organizational homology concept" shows that the discordances between genetic and morphological evolution are more prevalent than appreciated.[67] He believes that to understand these characteristic features of morphological evolution, scientists must consider processes and mechanisms beyond the realm of genetics.[68]

Müller identified three steps in the origination of homology that requires a causal explanation. These are "(1) the generation of initial parts and innovations; (2) the fixation of such new elements in the body plan of a phylogenetic lineage; and (3) the autonomization of homologues as process-independent elements of organismal design."[69] Müller and Newman write that all three chapters in this section, "Remind us that a number of distinct questions about the morphological phenomena of evolution remain unanswered.

---

63. Müller and Newman, *Organismal Form*, 12.
64. Morris, "Cambrian 'Explosion' of Metazoans," 27.
65. Müller and Newman, *Organismal Form*, 12.
66. Willmer, "Convergence and Homoplasy," 45.
67. Müller and Newman, *Organismal Form*, 12.
68. Müller and Newman, *Organismal Form*, 12.
69. Müller and Newman, *Organismal Form*, 12.

Notably, how did homoplasy, homology, and particular structural themes, including entire body plans, originate?"[70]

2.4 Scholars That Strongly Hold to Neo-Darwinism

Richard Dawkins is one of the leading evolutionary biologists in the world (see Figure 3). Dawkins holds a strong commitment to neo-Darwinism being a scientific fact. He once wrote in a book review, "It is absolutely safe to say that if you meet somebody who claims not to believe in evolution, that person is ignorant, stupid or insane (or wicked, but I'd rather not consider that)."[71]

In his *The Blind Watchmaker*, Dawkins compares William Paley's watchmaker analogy. Dawkins argues that the appearance of design in the world is not actually designed by a designer but is a product of an unguided mechanism called natural selection, which produces the life seen today through random mutation and time. He writes, "Biology is the study of complicated things that give the appearance of having been designed for a purpose."[72]

Unlike Thomas Nagel, Dawkins believes that Darwin made it possible to be an intellectually fulfilled atheist.[73] Not only that, he believes that Darwinism is the *only* known theory that is capable of explaining certain aspects of life.[74] While Dawkins says these things, he also says that Darwinism "requires effort of the *imagination* to escape from the prison of familiar timescale."[75]

Unlike Michael Ruse and Alister McGrath, Dawkins believes Darwinism can encompass all life. He writes, "It provides the only satisfying explanation for why we all exist, why we are the way that we are. It is the bedrock on which rest all the

---

70. Müller and Newman, *Organismal Form*, 12.
71. Dawkins, "In Short."
72. Dawkins, *Blind Watchmaker*, 4.
73. Dawkins, *Blind Watchmaker*, 10.
74. Dawkins, *Blind Watchmaker*, 406.
75. Dawkins, *Blind Watchmaker*, preface.

disciplines known as the humanities."[76] Also, contrary to Thomas Nagel, Dawkins holds to reductionism, but argues that he is not a nonexistent reductionist. This is where one tries to explain complicated things in the smallest parts.[77]

Instead, Dawkins is a hierarchal reductionist that describes "a complex entity at any particular level in the hierarchy of the organization, in terms of entities only one level down the hierarchy; entities which, themselves, are likely to be complex enough to need further reducing to their own component parts; and so on."[78] Dawkins does not believe that in order to understand how something works, it must be taken apart into the smallest unit, but rather, he thinks it should be taken apart one "level" at a time.

When it comes to the information argument, Dawkins proposes his famous monkey and Shakespeare example where he hypothesizes that with enough time, monkeys can produce a line of Shakespeare's "methinks it is a weasel" with a typewriter with a restricted keyboard, one with just twenty-six letters and a space bar.[79] He calculates that this would take over forty generations to accomplish.[80] Dawkins argues that, like this model, with enough time, genetic mutations can possibly result in the complexity we see in life today. Lennox, Gitt, Meyer, Sanford, and Berlinski all reject this hypothesis.

Similar to Dawkins's thinking, Professor of Philosophy Daniel Dennett has a similar take on neo-Darwinism. In his *Darwin's Dangerous Idea,* Dennett says, "To put it bluntly but fairly, anyone today who doubts that the variety of life on this planet was produced by a process of evolution is simply ignorant—inexcusably ignorant, in a world where three out of four people have learned to read and write."[81]

---

76. Dawkins, *Blind Watchmaker,* introduction.
77. Dawkins, *Blind Watchmaker,* 21.
78. Dawkins, *Blind Watchmaker,* 21.
79. Dawkins, *Blind Watchmaker,* 69.
80. Dawkins, *Blind Watchmaker,* 69.
81. Dennett, *Darwin's Dangerous Idea,* 46.

A SUMMARY OF NEO-DARWINIAN SCHOLARSHIP

When it comes to scientific theory, Dennett agrees with the Christian scholars that science needs philosophical presuppositions. He writes, "There is no such thing as philosophy-free science; there is only science whose philosophical baggage is taken on board without examination. The Darwinian Revolution is both a scientific and a philosophical revolution, and neither revolution could have occurred without the other."[82] In terms of the causes, Dennett does not see the need for God to be the cause of essential things. He thinks that excellence, worth, and purpose can come from a mindless, purposeless force.[83]

Evolutionary biologist Ernst Mayr believed that evolution was no longer a theory but as much as similar to the fact that the earth revolves around the sun.[84] He suspected that the changes documented by the fossil record in the geological strata go with evolution. He writes, "It is the factual basis on which the other four evolutionary theories rest. For instance, all the phenomena explained by common descent would make no sense if evolution were not a fact."[85] Unlike William Dembski, Mayr believed that chance is the ultimate explanation for natural selection. He writes, "Chance plays a role not only during the first step of natural selection, the production of new, genetically unique individuals, but also during the probabilistic process of the determination of the reproductive success of these individuals."[86]

Michael Ruse, philosopher of science, believes that evolution is beyond a reasonable doubt.[87] He also believes that Darwinism, as a genuine science, cannot answer the questions of meaning and purpose. He states, "If Darwinian thinking is to be turned from straight science into a kind of religion, it asks about the new ingredient."[88] He also holds to methodological natural-

---

82. Dennett, *Darwin's Dangerous Idea*, 21.
83. Dennett, *Darwin's Dangerous Idea*, 66.
84. Mayr and Kottler, "Darwin's Five Theories," 758.
85. Mayr and Kottler, "Darwin's Five Theories," 758.
86. Mayr and Kottler, "Darwin's Five Theories," 772.
87. Ruse, "Darwinism," 25.
88. Ruse, *Meaning to Life*, 99.

ism, stating, "One must explain the adaptedness of organisms by natural means."[89]

Like Dawkins, Ruse believes organisms work and function as if they are designed but does not suggest they are or are not designed.[90] Instead, he thinks the idea of a Designer who became involved miraculously in the process of evolution is inappropriate in the context of science.[91] However, Ruse also acknowledges that at the time of writing *On the Origin of Species*, Darwin had no direct evidence of selection.[92] Ruse differs from Müller and Newman in that the evidence of morphology is convincing for Darwinism. However, Ruse's thoughts on scientific theory are similar to those of Christian scholars where he writes, "Science will not work without rules, and experience tell us which are the best rules."[93]

In light of the morphological issues, Stephen Jay Gould's most famous work was his book, *Punctuated Equilibrium*, in 1972. Gould was a paleontologist and evolutionary biologist. He argued that the explosion of life in the Cambrian period was due to stasis (inactivity) rather than gradualism. Gould claims that Darwin was wrong by falsely assuming that the "slowness" of modification in domesticated animals or crop plants, as measured in ordinary human time, would translate into geological time as the continuation and slowness of phyletic gradualism.[94] He writes that there is an "observed high relative frequency of stasis during the full geological range of metazoan species preserved in the fossil record."[95] Dawkins finds punctuated equilibrium to be a minor variety of Darwinism and not a rival theory.[96]

On the contrary, Müller, Newman, Berlinski, and Meyer see the Cambrian era findings to be problematic for the

89. Ruse, "Darwinism," 26.
90. Ruse, "Darwinism," 27.
91. Ruse, "Darwinism," 27.
92. Ruse, *Charles Darwin*, 75.
93. Ruse, "Darwinism," 23.
94. Gould, *Punctuated Equilibrium*, 40.
95. Gould, *Punctuated Equilibrium*, 175.
96. Dawkins, *Blind Watchmaker*, 405.

neo-Darwinian paradigm. Despite Gould's position on punctuated equilibrium, Gould admits that the scientific evidence of evolution does not trump the possibility of God interacting with life via evolutionary processes. He writes:

> To say it for all my colleagues and for the umpteenth millionth time (from college bull sessions to learned treatises): science simply cannot (by its legitimate methods) adjudicate the issue of God's possible superintendence of nature. We neither affirm nor deny it; we simply can't comment on it as scientists. If some of our crowd have made untoward statements claiming that Darwinism disproves God, then I will find Mrs. McInerney[97] and have their knuckles rapped for it (as long as she can equally treat those members of our crowd who have argued that Darwinism must be God's method of action). Science can work only with naturalistic explanations; it can neither affirm nor deny other types of actors (like God) in other spheres (the moral realm, for example).[98]

Despite the seeming dilemmas, evolutionary biologist Richard Lewontin admits to holding on to *a priori* assumptions regarding neo-Darwinism despite a lack of evidence. Quoted earlier in this review, Lewontin made it clear that the world of science must hold to material causes despite the evidence against it in order to avoid allowing a Divine Foot in the door of science.[99] This is in contrast to Thomas Henry Huxley, a champion for Darwinism, who tried to hold to a neutral view of science by stating that science "commits suicide when it adopts a creed."[100]

Philosopher of Science Sandy C. Boucher is an advocate for methodological naturalism in the sciences. He challenges Alvin Plantinga's argument against methodological naturalism. Boucher believes there is no blatant and drawn-out line dividing the supernatural and natural. He notes, "The concepts of the natural

---

97. Gould's third grade math teacher.
98. Gould and Johnson, "Impeaching," 119.
99. Lewontin, "Billions and Billions."
100. Huxley, "Darwin Memorial," 252.

and the supernatural are in fact hopelessly obscure, such that the claim that science is committed to methodological naturalism cannot be made good."[101]

Boucher believes that "supernatural theories could become a legitimate part of science (as they arguably have been in the past) if the evidence in their favor were sufficiently convincing. There is nothing inherently unscientific about supernaturalist theories."[102] In addition, he believes that inferences to intelligent design are intelligible and could potentially count as scientific, but he believes the inference to be supernatural or divine intelligent design is not intelligible or scientific because we can attach no sense to the notion of the supernatural.[103] Unlike Thomas Nagel, Boucher thinks that the arguments of creationists or Intelligent Designers are overwhelmingly negative because they are criticisms of the supposed inadequacies of neo-Darwinian theory and provide limited positive evidence in their own respective favor.[104]

Thomas Huxley's grandson and evolutionary biologist, Julian Huxley, believed that evolution is "the most powerful and the most comprehensive idea that has ever arisen on earth."[105] Julian held to the idea that the evolutionary outlook must be scientific.[106] Julian seems to have a different outlook than Michael Ruse in the context of what Darwinism tells us. Julian believes evolutionary ideas help the human race understand itself as unique organisms equipped with "a new method of evolution" that he calls cultural evolution, which is based on the summative transmission of experience through language and symbols.[107] However, he claimed that Darwinism accepted the desirability of change and

---

101. Boucher, "Methodological Naturalism," abstract.
102. Boucher, "Methodological Naturalism," 58.
103. Boucher, "Methodological Naturalism," 71.
104. Boucher, "Methodological Naturalism," 78.
105. Huxley, *Essays of a Humanist*, 125.
106. Huxley, *Essays of a Humanist*, 84.
107. Huxley, *Essays of a Humanist*, 127.

advancement by welcoming a new discovery even when it conflicts with old traditional ways of thinking.[108]

Julian wanted evolution to be the new means of thinking, a new framework of values or ideology, that would grow and develop in the light of the "new evolutionary vision."[109] Interestingly enough, Julian was once asked on television why evolution was accepted so quickly. He said, "The reason we accepted Darwinism even without proof, is because we didn't want God to interfere with our sexual mores."[110]

This chapter has covered the competing perspectives among leading scientist and philosophers about the neo-Darwinian paradigm. What was found is that a particular worldview does not necessarily generate an exclusive view on neo-Darwinism. It was shown that there are highly intelligent and qualified Christians, non-Christian, and even atheists who find interpretative issues and differences with the scientific evidence for neo-Darwinism. However, it was also shown that there are still highly intelligent and qualified scientists and philosophers that believe the evidence is highly in favor of neo-Darwinism. This contention was highlighted and synthesized to show that if there are highly intelligent and qualified scholars from various perspectives disagreeing on the veridicality and veracity of neo-Darwinian conclusions, then one may ponder whether there might be another reason for this conflict of thought.

---

108. Huxley, *Essays of a Humanist*, 84.
109. Huxley, *Essays of a Humanist*, 83.
110. Kennedy, *Skeptics Answered*, epilogue.

Scholars That Strongly Hold to Neo-Darwinism

Name	Worldview	Rationale
Richard Dawkins	Atheism	Cumulative selection may explain the possibility for genetic mutations resulting in the complexity of life.
Daniel Dennett	Atheism	Science and philosophy are contingent upon each other.
Ernst Mayr	Atheism	The theory of common descent explains the phenomena of complexity we see today.
Michael Ruse	Atheism	Natural explanations provide adequate evidence for the adaptivity of organisms.
Stephen J. Gould	Atheism	The abrupt appearance of species in the Cambrian period can be explained by a period of stasis followed by an explosion of life.
Richard Lewontin	Atheism	Science must not allow a Divine foot in the door of science.
Sandy Boucher	Atheism	One cannot attach the notion of the "supernatural" in a scientific context.
Julian Huxley	Atheism	Evolutionary theories provide exhaustive explanatory power and scope for all manner of life.

Figure 3 © Alexander J. Bonitto, 2023

3

A Careful Consideration of Methodological Approach

THE MAIN CONCERN OF this book is to weigh the five *a priori* assumptions of neo-Darwinism utilizing the same standards that the proponents of neo-Darwinism recommend. This brief chapter will explain the methodology used to collect, analyze, and draw inferences for the conclusions made in this book.

3.1 Data Collection

This book's investigation rests/relies upon meta-analyses of numerous scientific books, articles, reports, studies, and discussions undertaken by leading scientists and philosophers in evolutionary thought. Thus, works that address the topic of neo-Darwinism as a whole and works that address the five specific *a priori* assumptions for neo-Darwinian conclusions were collected and synthesized.

Books and articles by the leading minds of evolutionary biology were the main pieces of literature. Primary sources of Charles Darwin and Alfred Wallace were used to get an accurate definition of original Darwinism. Additionally, a chronological investigation of literature directing evolutionary biologists was used to grasp a holistic definition of neo-Darwinism. Additionally, the best and strongest definitions of neo-Darwinism were used to prevent a strawman fallacy against neo-Darwinism, itself.

Furthermore, some video documentaries and written testimonies were analyzed to capture the dialogue between opposing views of neo-Darwinism and theism. Literature from five different perspectives on neo-Darwinism was collected. These five different perspectives were the following:

1. Atheistic and non-Christian scientists and philosophers that believe in neo-Darwinism.
2. Atheistic and non-Christian scientists and philosophers that do not believe in neo-Darwinism.
3. Christian scientists and philosophers that believe in Creationism.
4. Christian scientists and philosophers that believe in Intelligent Design.
5. Theistic evolutionists.

These pieces of literature were gathered in a few ways. Online academic databases were utilized for the majority of data collection of primary sources. Sources in the bibliography of the primary sources were utilized as well. Books and articles that were helpful but are not accessible from these databases were purchased by personal expense in either hardcopy, kindle version, or other electronic versions.

3.2 Data Analysis Technique

All sources were compiled into a literature matrix wherein each column was a separate source and each row was a specific topic based on what was found when reading through the sources. This allowed all different findings and opinions on certain subjects to be adjacent to each other with their respective categories. The results and conclusion for each perspective were analyzed with sources from the five different perspectives of neo-Darwinism. The notes gleaned from each source were put into their respective categories, and each piece of content was contrasted to find differences and similarities. Then, contradictions and corroborations were searched for in sources from each of the five individual perspectives on neo-Darwinism. Internal contradictions and corroborations were noted and highlighted in the literature matrix within each respective viewpoint.

3.3 Adjudication Philosophy

Preceding the data collection, the five *a priori* assumptions of neo-Darwinism were examined to determine their veridicality. The standards that atheist and non-Christian scientists/philosophers used to claim that neo-Darwinism is true were utilized to determine the five necessary *a priori* assumptions of neo-Darwinism. This was done purposefully to strengthen the argument of this book. This book would make a much weaker argument if it only used the adjudicating standards of a Creationist or Intelligent Designer.

Two different standards were used to adjudicate the five neo-Darwinian *a priori* assumptions because certain concepts would not apply to a certain standard. Note that all the adjudicating standards at times mingle among these bifurcated standards. This is normal and provides appropriate nuance to the neo-Darwinian *a priori* assumptions. For most of the analyses, the following standards were used.

The first standard of adjudication was the scientific method. According to C. George Thomas, the following actions[1] are required when utilizing the scientific method:

1. Make observations or gather information
2. Develop a hypothesis
3. Predict results
4. Design an experiment

1. Thomas, *Research Methodology*, 26.

5. Conduct the experiment and collect data
6. Evaluation and conclusion
7. Acceptance, modification, or rejection of the hypothesis

This standard was used to adjudicate two of the five neo-Darwinian *a priori* assumptions. These were the micro-evolutionary to macro-evolutionary assumption and methodological naturalism. The micro-evolutionary to macro-evolutionary assumption is in this category because it is claimed to be based on empirical data by neo-Darwinists. Methodological naturalism is in this category because it contends against the empirical evidence found in the postulations of information and intelligence.

The other three neo-Darwinian *a priori* assumptions—gradualism, tree of life hypothesis, and time and chance—were weighed based on different criteria because they are forensic and cannot be tested, empirically. The following criteria used to adjudicate these concepts are explanatory power, use of ad hoc, and explanatory scope.

Explanatory Power accounts for information while diminishing the amount of vagueness or obscurity. It accounts for the falsifiability of a theory that asks whether it can be easily tested or disproven. If it cannot and instead rests on an assumption with no correlating or causal evidence, then it lacks explanatory power. Similarly, not using ad hoc solutions prevents fallacious new beliefs from being formed that try to "fit in" a theory with no independent evidence. Stephen Jay Gould's punctuated equilibrium and Richard Dawkins's hypothesis that aliens seeded life on Earth would fit into this category of ad hoc solutions. We want to diminish these to develop an inference grounded in obtainable knowledge.

Furthermore, *Explanatory Scope* has to do with the number of things it explains and why these particular things are true. If a theory can explain a higher number of things, then it has more explanatory scope. These three standards will aid in the adjudication of the plausibility of the *a priori* assumptions of neo-Darwinism.

3.4 Limitations

It is important to note that the purpose of this book is not to supply an exhaustive scientific refutation of neo-Darwinism but rather to critique the interpretive issues of the *a priori* assumptions neo-Darwinists must hold on to arrive at neo-Darwinian conclusions. Scientific literature is necessary for this book, but the main emphasis is the philosophical implication of the scientific findings since the science of neo-Darwinism is much more qualitative and philosophical than its quantitative cousins: chemistry and physics. In addition, this book does not give an exhaustive examination of the ramifications of neo-Darwinism, although the important ramifications are touched upon. Lastly, this book's main agenda is not to make a positive case for Intelligent Design but to provide a negative case for neo-Darwinism's censorship. Although positive arguments for Intelligent Design are utilized, they are not the focal point of this book.

The meta-analysis of this book collected literature from leading scientists and philosophers of evolutionary thought from five different perspectives on neo-Darwinism. It synthesized the findings to spot contradictions and corroborations among supporting and competing views. The information gleaned from these sources was adjudicated based on the scientific method, the level of explanatory power, the use of ad hoc, and the level of explanatory scope to determine the veridicality of the *a priori* assumptions of neo-Darwinism, which will be addressed in the next chapter.

4

Putting Neo-Darwinism to the Test

THE OBJECTIVE OF THIS chapter is not to give an exhaustive scientific refutation of neo-Darwinism, but to "put a stone in the shoe" of a neo-Darwinist by challenging the validity of the *a priori* assumptions necessary for neo-Darwinian conclusions. By this means, the predicament is not necessarily the study of neo-Darwinism but its pontification. The beginning section will continue the discussion from chapter one on the relationship between *a priori* assumptions in scientific theory and neo-Darwinism.

4.1 A *Priori* Assumptions, Scientific Theory, and Neo-Darwinism

One can dichotomize the sciences into two main categories: quantitative and qualitative. *A priori* assumptions play a crucial and appropriate role in these sciences because both rely on *a priori* assumptions to shape how the data is interpreted to some extent. However, quantitative sciences generally hold more authority because they are more empirical than qualitative sciences. Sciences like chemistry and physics fall in this category. The linchpin of quantitative sciences is the laws of nature.

Werner Gitt says, "If the truth of a statement is verified repeatedly in a reproducible way so that it is regarded as generally valid, then we have a natural law."[1] The caveat, however, is that the laws of nature cannot be proved within 100 percent of certainty. However, they can be identified and quantified through observation.[2] Therefore, one must assume *a priori* that the laws of nature will work when constructing experiments. Interestingly, many laws of nature are descriptive (not explanatory) inasmuch as describing regularities rather than explaining why the events they described occur.[3]

Newton's Universal Law of Gravitation is a great example. As Stephen Meyer puts it, "The fundamental laws of physics describe mathematically but do not explain the *phenomena* they cover."[4] In addition to the laws of nature, the laws of logic must be assumed *a priori* to carry out a scientific study. This means that since both the laws of nature and the laws of logic are utilized in science, they cannot be the result of them.

In qualitative sciences, *a priori* assumptions are relied on much more. This is because the *a priori* assumptions fundamentally shape how the data is interpreted. This is where theories and hypotheses come into play in science. Theories are scientific statements based on empirical findings.[5] Since the provisional nature of theories rarely have empirical results, they can be made in terms of specific inductive probabilities in the best case.[6] Thus, theories must compare the explanatory power of other competing

---

1. Gitt, *In the Beginning*, 22.
2. Gitt, *In the Beginning*, 26–27.
3. Meyer, "Darwinism, Science or Philosophy?" 30.
4. Meyer, "Laws, Causes, and Facts," 30.
5. Gitt, *In the Beginning*, 23.
6. Gitt, *In the Beginning*, 23.

hypotheses or theories.[7] The best theories are those that contain the least number of inconsistencies.[8]

Consequently, a working theory or hypothesis should be abandoned if it is faced with facts or empirical findings that defy every attempt at rational explanation.[9] This does not mean that qualitative sciences are not valid studies. Stephen Meyer says, "Many scientific explanations depend primarily upon antecedent causal conditions and events, not laws, to do . . . explanatory work."[10] This is because if investigators limit themselves to a stringent empirical account for science (as Alister McGrath says), "We fail to appreciate its full meaning, value, or agency."[11] This means that philosophy must play a role to get the fullness of science.

Daniel Dennett brilliantly says, "There is no such thing as philosophy-free science; there is only science whose philosophical baggage is taken on board without examination."[12] So, it is possible to have an Intelligent-Designist (Meyer), a theistic-evolutionist (McGrath), and a neo-Darwinist (Dennett) all agreeing that philosophy plays a role in the study of science. However, many neo-Darwinists seem to place neo-Darwinism in a more quantitative category rather than qualitative.

Richard Dawkins writes that neo-Darwinism is "indeed, a remarkably simple theory; childishly so, one would have thought, in comparison with almost all of physics and mathematics."[13] Julian Huxley remarked, "Evolution—or, to spell it out, the idea of the evolutionary process—is the most powerful and the most comprehensive idea that has ever arisen on earth."[14] Ernst Mayr says, "Evolution as such is no longer a theory for a modern author. It is as much a fact as that the earth revolves around the sun rather than the

---

7. Meyer, "Laws, Causes, and Facts," 34.
8. Gitt, *In the Beginning*, 23.
9. Lennox, *God's Undertaker*, 34.
10. Meyer, "Laws, Causes, and Facts," 30.
11. McGrath, *Darwinism and the Divine*, 11–12.
12. Dennett, *Darwin's Dangerous Idea*, 21.
13. Dawkins, *Blind Watchmaker*, preface.
14. Huxley, *Essays of a Humanist*, 125.

reverse."[15] The problem with these statements is that, unlike facts, theories have the property of consilience or agreement.[16]

Contrary to the mentioned examples, David Hull admits, "Very few of the elements of the synthetic theory of evolution are connected deductively."[17] Additionally, Gerd Müller believes the study of morphological structures is "foremost a qualitative property."[18] So, which one does neo-Darwinism fall under?

The forensic nature of the neo-Darwinian paradigm places it in a qualitative science because the origin of life cannot be tested, repeatably. Yet, if it cannot be tested, is it truly a science based on the scientific method? Neo-Darwinism attempts to answer the question, "How did life begin?" and "What mechanism brought it about?" So, due to the qualitative nature of neo-Darwinian theory, it relies on *a priori* assumptions to *fundamentally* shape how the data is interpreted. The question is whether these assumptions are appropriate like others that are utilized in quantitative sciences, which themselves rely on *a priori* assumptions—e.g., the laws of logic and laws of nature.

The following sections will develop a case on whether the *a priori* assumptions for neo-Darwinism are supported and convincing (See Figure 2). The upcoming section will dive into the evidence of the fossil record discovered in the Burgess Shale and explain why its findings are incongruent with the *a priori* assumptions of gradualism and the tree of life hypothesis (both of which are crucial for neo-Darwinian theory).

15. Mayr and Kottler, "Darwin's Five Theories," 758.
16. Meyer, "Laws, Causes, and Facts," 36.
17. Hull and Kottler, "Darwinism as a Historical Entity," 806.
18. Müller, "Homology," 54.

Neo-Darwinian A Priori Analyses					
Neo-Darwinian A Priori Assumptions	Gradualism	Tree of Life Hypothesis	Micro-Macro Hypothesis	Time and Chance Hypothesis	Methodological Naturalism
What They Are	All life has evolved via a long process of small and minute steps in the direction of simple to more complex.	All life came from a single-parent organism and that lineage can be traced via an interconnected tree of life.	Empirical evidence observed for micro evolution can further correlate to the macro transitioning of species.	With enough time, there is a plausible chance that genetic mutations can account for the complexity of functioning organisms known today.	All scientific theories must explain any and all phenomena via material causes.
Rationale For Them	Larger changes that result in new species are a result of the succession of smaller incremental steps.	Deep divergence hypothesis and the universal genetic code.	Enough adaptations observed at the micro level can eventually account for larger macro changes (similar to gradualism).	Cumulative selection elicits a higher probability (Dawkins' "Methinks it is like a weasel" example).	Inferences to supernatural causes cannot be considered scientific because scientists cannot attach a sense to the notion of the "supernatural." There is no sufficient evidence in favor of the supernatural.
Why They Don't Work	Evidence of the Cambrian Explosion reveals an abrupt arrival of complex organisms.	Taxonomy issues show that evolutionary trees from different genes have conflicting patterns. Genomic potential hypothesis reveals that if life originated from chemicals, it would result in a "lawn" of life rather than a "tree" of life.	Irreducibly complex systems would create a non-viability for transitioning life forms. Genetic limits are empirically observed within Escherichia coli bacteria and Drosophila fruit flies. Darwin observed adaptations of Galapagos finches to be constrained by a back-and-forth cycle of variable adaptations.	Cumulative selection is not blind and purposeless; therefore, it does not represent the true definition of natural selection. The probability of a blind and purposeless mechanism accounting for the complexity of life is 1 in 10^{77}.	Many scientific explanations depend on cause instead of laws for explanatory work. Presupposing that materials can be the only cause neglects other possible scientific models for agency— i.e., information and the immaterial mind.

Figure 4 © Alexander J. Bonitto, 2023

4.2 The Cambrian 'Explosion'

4.2.1 Gradualism

Gradualism assumes that evolutionary transformation always proceeds gradually, *never* in jumps.[19] Charles Darwin stated, "No complex instinct can possibly be produced through natural selection, except by the slow and gradual accumulation of numerous slight, profitable variations."[20] However, he realized that the distinctness of specific forms is not being blended together by innumerable transitional links, bringing undeniable difficulty into his premise.[21] This was before the findings of the Burgess Shale in British Columbia in 1909 by Charles Doolittle Walcott.

This fossil site contains numerous unique and complex animals throughout several phyla. The fossils are dated to be within

19. Mayr and Kottler, "Darwin's Five Theories," 761.
20. Darwin, *On the Origin*, 197.
21. Darwin, *On the Origin*, 260.

the middle Cambrian era. The significance has to do with the abrupt arrival of complex organisms. This coined its term, "Cambrian Explosion," having to do with the dramatic emergence of new life forms. Rather than the number of new phyla discovered, the Cambrian explosion confers a conundrum for evolutionary biologists due to the immense number of new and unique animal forms and structures that seem to have arisen "out of thin air."[22]

Stephen Meyer notes that the Burgess Shale and any other series of sedimentary strata known in Walcott's day recorded a fossil patterning that resembles a gradual sequence of intermediates.[23] On the contrary, these sedimentary strata seem to reveal completely unique organisms like the strange arthropod *Opabinia*, which has "fifteen articulated body segments, twenty-eight gills, thirty flipper-like swimming lobes, long trunk-like proboscis, intricate nervous system, and five separate eyes"—where all seem to have appeared fully formed in the Cambrian strata, thus contradicting the assumption of gradualism.[24]

In *Origination of Organismal Form*, Gerd Müller and Stuart Newman have responded to this seeming contradiction with gradualism. They state, "If, as we suggest, the failure of the current theory of evolution to deal with the problem of origination is the major obstacle to a scientific understanding of organismal form, it is incumbent on us to provide at least a sketch of an alternative view."[25] A section in their discussion, "Problems with Morphological Evolution," delves into these problems of origination of the neo-Darwinian Paradigm.

Within this section, Simon Conway Morris hypothesizes that if Charles Darwin returned today, his suspicion articulated in chapter nine of *On the Origin of Species*, that the seemingly abrupt appearance of skeletons near the beginning of the Cambrian, would undermine his notion of gradualism.[26]

22. Meyer, *Darwin's Doubt*, 33.
23. Meyer, *Darwin's Doubt*, 36.
24. Meyer, *Darwin's Doubt*, 36.
25. Müller and Newman, *Organismal Form*, 8.
26. Morris, "Cambrian 'Explosion,'" 27.

On the contrary, Richard Dawkins argues that the complexity we see in life forms today cannot be explained as originating from a single step.[27] Meyer notes that some scientists have claimed that the Precambrian fossils had not been found yet and that the incomplete sampling of the fossil record is the reason. In contrast, others suggest the Precambrian sedimentary rock did not preserve the missing fossils because they were too small, soft, or both to be preserved.[28] The problem with these conclusions is that they are educated-but-still-biased guesses. Their summations are contrary to the raw evidence of the fossil record.

David Berlinski objects to alternate hypotheses made for the lack of evidence of gradualism as he writes, "If those 'major transitions' represent a 'sudden emergence of new forms,' the obvious conclusion to draw is not that nature is perverse, *but that Darwin was wrong*" [Italics added].[29] Harking back to what was stated earlier, "[A] working theory or hypothesis should be abandoned if it is faced with facts or empirical findings that defy every attempt at rational explanation."[30]

To account for the Burgess Shale findings, in 1972, paleontologist Stephen Jay Gould formulated a "new" theory in light of the explosion of new and complex lifeforms in the Cambrian era. In a more recent update, Gould says, "Punctuated equilibrium holds that the great majority of species, as evidenced by their anatomical and geographical histories in the fossil record, originate in geological moments (punctuations) and then persist in stasis throughout their long durations."[31]

In simpler terms, punctuated equilibrium is supposed to account for the rapid appearance of complex lifeforms found during the Cambrian period and hypothesizes that, in nature, stasis (a period of inactivity) happens for a long time, then punctuations happen where lifeforms arise, then it goes back to stasis.

27. Dawkins, *Blind Watchmaker*, 22.
28. Meyer, *Darwin's Doubt*, 56.
29. Berlinski, *Devil's Delusion*, 192.
30. Lennox, *God's Undertaker*, 34.
31. Gould, *Punctuated Equilibrium*, 40.

The most crucial ground rule of punctuated equilibrium is that it claims to appeal to dominate patterns rather than an assertion of the existence of a phenomenon.[32] However, Gould never reveals the contingent phenomena of the "missing" transitions that Darwin claimed to have explained.[33]

Interestingly, Morris accuses Gould of a "strange materialist agenda" by arguing that a fortuitous cause for the origin of humans leads to certain ethical consequences.[34] However, whatever agenda Gould has does not mean his proclamation is false. The vital problem with his punctuated equilibrium is not his agenda but that no new data was found to support his new conclusion. The *a priori* assumption was simply changed to interpret the same data. If qualitative sciences utilize empirical evidence to formulate new theories, then new empirical evidence should be discovered when generating new theories.

In Gould's case, there was none. The assertions of stasis and punctuation may be accurate, and they seem to correlate better than the inconsistencies with gradualism; however, at best, it is a well-educated guess.

4.2.2 Tree of Life Hypothesis

Gradualism and the tree of life hypothesis are interconnected. Gradualism is an antecedent assumption for the tree of life hypothesis to work. With the sudden appearance of life during the Cambrian period, one might conclude that if investigators do not have fossils documenting a gradual progression, there must be some other explanation. The deep divergence hypothesis is a central explanation used to negate this sudden appearance of new complex life.

---

32. Gould, *Punctuated Equilibrium*, 40.
33. Berlinski, *Devil's Delusion*, 188.
34. Morris, "Cambrian 'Explosion,'" 22.

4.2.2.1 Deep Divergence

The deep divergence hypothesis uses genetic studies to account for the branching of animal species to resemble the tree of life. Richard Dawkins asserts that since there is a universal genetic code, it can be regarded as "near-conclusive proof that all organisms are descended from a single common ancestor."[35] In addition, Daniel Dennett asserts,

> There is no serious controversy about the fact that all the diversity of life that has ever existed on this planet is derived from this single fan-out; the controversies arise about how to discover and describe in general terms the various forces, principles, constraints, etc., that permit us to give a scientific explanation of the patterns in all this diversity.[36]

The problem with these statements is that there is a considerable amount of controversy among the scientific community about how the tree of life should be classified and what it should look like.

Since evolutionary history only happened once, and the trees of life illustrate the hypotheses of the unobserved relationships between animal groups, then if there are two or more conflicting hypotheses, the tree of life has not been figured out because there is only one history.[37] James Degnan and Noah Rosenberg published a paper in *Trends in Ecology and Evolution* recognizing that evolutionary trees from different genes often have conflicting branching patterns.[38] Meyer gives three reasons for this:

1. Comparisons of different molecules repeatedly generate divergent trees.
2. Comparison of anatomical characteristics and molecules repeatedly produced divergent trees.

---

35. Dawkins, *Blind Watchmaker*, 383.
36. Dennett, *Darwin's Dangerous Idea*, 86.
37. Meyer, *Darwin's Doubt*, 117.
38. Degnan and Rosenberg, "Gene Tree Discordance," 332.

3. Trees based only on different anatomical characteristics often contradict each other.[39]

Furthermore, biologist Eugene Koonin has observed that there are major transitions in biological evolution that show an identical pattern of a sudden emergence of diverse forms at a new level of complexity.[40] He says the relationships between major groups within an emerging new class of biological entities are "hard to decipher and do not seem to fit the tree pattern that Darwin's originally proposed."[41]

These biological entities include the origin of complex RNA molecules and protein folds, major groups of viruses, archaea and bacteria, and the dominant lineages within each of these prokaryotic domains; eukaryotic supergroups; and animal phyla.[42] He notes that these entities seem to have appeared rapidly and fully equipped with the signature features of the respective new level of biological organization. He further states, "No intermediate 'grades' or intermediate forms between different types are detectable."[43]

Additionally, Liliana Dávalos and her fellow researchers assert that this phylogenetic conflict is common and is routinely the norm rather than the exception.[44] A notable study by Michael Syvanen analyzed two thousand genes in six animals that span diverse phyla like the chordates, echinoderms, arthropods, and nematodes.[45] His analysis consequently did not yield a tree-like pattern.[46] The evidence was so blatantly not in favor of the tree of life hypothesis that Syvanen exclaimed, "We've just annihilated the tree of life. It's not a tree anymore; it is a different topology entirely.

---

39. Meyer, *Darwin's Doubt*, 119.
40. Koonin, "Biological Big Bang," abstract.
41. Koonin, "Biological Big Bang," abstract.
42. Koonin, "Biological Big Bang," abstract.
43. Koonin, "Biological Big Bang," abstract.
44. Dávalos et al., "Phylogenetic Incongruence," 993.
45. Meyer, *Darwin's Doubt*, 119.
46. Meyer, *Darwin's Doubt*, 119.

What would Darwin have made of that?"[47] With all these challenges, one may argue that these trees at least show "some type" of tree-like pattern preceding the Cambrian period; however, this is simply because they assume *a priori* that there must be a tree of life. There is no demonstration of it.[48]

4.2.2.2 Genomic Potential Hypothesis

Additionally, Christian Schwabe argues from a chemistry standpoint that if life originated from chemicals, it would not result in one common ancestor but rather a slew of lifeforms coming into existence at one time. It is more of a "lawn" of life rather than a "tree" of life. He explains that the neo-Darwinian mechanism of natural selection acting on random genetic mutations that produce the top-down pattern that scientists observe in the history of life following the Cambrian explosion should not be expected.[49]

Schwabe argues that there are no intermediate forms in the fossil record because mutations cannot be a mechanism to produce new organisms; thus, the evolutionary trees that are presented are images created by the sequential ripening of proforms and their rapid rise into the fossil scene.[50] Schwabe bluntly asserts that there was never a time on earth when only one kind or species existed.[51]

The formation of new and distinct species via a slow gradual process (speciation) seems to have never been substantiated by plausible evidence. All examples of speciation found in the literature today are all a postulation *"inspired by the hypothesis."*[52] This means that speciation is derived from an ad hoc hypothesis that uses its conclusion to shape the way the evidence is interpreted. So, the standard line of thinking that: if animals A and B have certain features in

---

47. Lawton, "Why Darwin Was Wrong," 39.
48. Meyer, *Darwin's Doubt*, 133.
49. Meyer, *Darwin's Doubt*, 43.
50. Schwabe, *Genomic Potential Hypothesis*, 2.
51. Schwabe, *Genomic Potential Hypothesis*, 43.
52. Schwabe, *Genomic Potential Hypothesis*, 43.

common, then they, therefore, are derived from a common ancestor, is *"merely a restatement of the parent hypothesis."*[53]

4.2.2.3 Genetic Commonalities

Neo-Darwinists also assume that the commonality of every life-form containing the universal genetic code is an obvious explanation for common ancestry. The rationale for this assumption is the 99 percent genetic commonality between apes and humans. The problem with this assumption is that the similarity of the gross contents of the genetic code cannot always account for its order. Consider the two statements: "Goku is a martial arts god" and "Goku is a martial arts dog."[54]

The two statements contain 100 percent of the same information, and the characters are worded 92.3 percent the same; however, they have two completely different meanings. In light of DNA, this creates a dilemma for the tree of life hypothesis because the sequence of nucleotide bases in DNA have much to do in determining its function. Variations in these sequences typically lead to dysfunction.[55] This is because any variation usually renders the protein dysfunctional.[56] To say that the similarity of the genetic code can provide a substantial inference to common ancestry is a fair postulation; however, with other things considered, it seems unconvincing.

In support of this objection, biochemist and convinced structuralist Michael Denton observed in 1985 that there were problems tracing the traditional evolutionary transition of animals at a molecular level: cyclostome → fish → amphibian → reptile → mammal.[57] So, the traditional consideration of amphibia, an intermediate between fish and other terrestrial vertebrates, is incorrect.[58]

53. Schwabe, *Genomic Potential Hypothesis*, 43.
54. Geisler and Turek, *Don't Have Enough Faith*, 150.
55. Email correspondence with the author, Feb. 2, 2024.
56. Geisler and Turek, *Don't Have Enough Faith*, 150.
57. Denton, *Evolution*, 284.
58. Denton, *Evolution*, 285.

In molecular terms, they are as far from fish as any group of reptiles or mammals.[59] Thirty-one years later, Denton still has yet to find any empirical evidence that would affirm some key neo-Darwinian principles. He writes, "I will show further that advances since 1985 are not supportive of Darwinian claims. On the contrary, the gaps or discontinuities alluded to in Evolution are 'as wide as ever,' especially when re-assessed from a structuralist perspective."[60] Simply put, the genetic commonalities are not a substantial assumption for an interconnecting tree of life.

4.2.2.4 Convergent Evolution

Convergent evolution argues that the similarities observed in animals do not always result from a common ancestry (homology). Pat Willmer notes that the developmental studies of the convergent origins are becoming clouded.[61] She says, "We still do not know enough about molecular genomic variation within phyla to be sure the very few representatives chosen thus far are typical or 'normal' for a particular taxon."[62] She believes that it may be impossible to maintain convergence that reaches out to the polyphyly of the animal kingdom; as she says, "The jury is still out."[63] Thus, there are many sources of change in the genome that may invalidate traditional assumptions about homology and the independence of characters.[64]

So, the convergence creates problems for similar designs without common ancestry. Instead of common genes accounting for common structures in fruit flies, worms, and mammals, scientists have concluded that genes influence the development of a certain "type" of structure that is "in the right place at the

---

59. Denton, *Evolution*, 285.
60. Denton, *Evolution*, 16.
61. Willmer, "Convergence and Homoplasy," 38.
62. Willmer, "Convergence and Homoplasy," 44.
63. Willmer, "Convergence and Homoplasy," 44.
64. Willmer, "Convergence and Homoplasy," 45.

right time."⁶⁵ The application of molecular taxonomy to the "big" problems of phyletic relationships has altered Willmer's views on where animals belong in the tree of life, and, as Willmer says, "How they must have evolved."⁶⁶

What is interesting about Wilmer's statement is that animals *must* evolve. This again seems to indicate that evolution is assumed *a priori*, thus, influencing how the data is interpreted. Why must they evolve? Perhaps the evidence for the adaptability observed in what is called micro-evolution is being attributed to macro-evolution.

4.3 Does Micro-Evolution Account for Macro-Evolution?

David Prindle accuses Creationists of relying on ill-informed presuppositions to back up their claim. He writes, "Creationism is a collection of vague, often contradictory, and sometimes nonsensical suppositions that generally are unable to generate empirically testable predictions, and on the few occasions when it has done so, these have not been supported."⁶⁷ He says this while there is no clear empirical evidence for the macro-evolutionary jump.

Ostensibly, it may not be fair to exclude macro-evolution because of this lack of evidence. As Francis Collins believes, the distinction between macro and micro-evolution is arbitrary.⁶⁸ Larger changes that result in new species are a result of a succession of smaller incremental steps.⁶⁹ This is a fair postulation; however, there seems to be empirical evidence that suggests *against* this. It starts with irreducible complexity.

---

65. Willmer, "Convergence and Homoplasy," 38.
66. Willmer, "Convergence and Homoplasy," 43.
67. Prindle, *Politics of Evolution*, 129.
68. Collins, *Language of God*, 132.
69. Collins, *Language of God*, 132.

4.3.1 Irreducible Complexity

Charles Darwin wrote, "If it could be demonstrated that any complex organ existed, which could not possibly have been formed by numerous, successive, slight modifications, my theory would absolutely break down."[70] Consequently, Michael Behe discovered the irreducible complexity of a cell. Irreducible complexity is a "single system composed of several well-matched, interacting parts that contribute to the basic function, wherein the removal of any one of the parts causes the system to cease function."[71] Behe notes that irreducibly complex systems cannot be produced directly by slight successive modifications of a precursor system because any missing precursor part to that irreducibly complex system will be considered nonfunctional.[72]

His famous example of an irreducibly complex system was the mousetrap. He argued that if one has a five-part mousetrap, and when one part of the mouse trap is missing, the whole thing will not work anymore. As mentioned in the literature view, Ken Miller disagreed with Behe's point by building a mousetrap with four parts on a televised debate on PBS. Behe responded that it only elicits the need for intelligence. Additionally, substituting the four parts does not negate the claim. He argued that if you take the mouse board out and use the floor, you are still using the floor as a board.

The problem with Miller's response is that it actually coincides with Behe's claim that all five parts are needed. You may combine one part or replace the part with something else, but the *function* must be there. All Miller did was push back the argument. He may be able to use the floor instead of the board, but that function that the board or the floor makes is needed no matter what. As Behe replies to his critics, "If one removes a part of a clearly defined, irreducibly complex system, the system itself immediately and necessarily ceases to function."[73]

70. Darwin, *On the Origin*, 177.
71. Behe, *Darwin's Black Box*, 42.
72. Behe, *Darwin's Black Box*, 42–3.
73. Behe, "Reply to My Critics," 693.

Additionally, on a macro level, this complexity argues for the non-viability of transitional life forms. Going back to the fossil record, scientists do not see transitional life forms in the fossil record. It is therefore plausible to believe that the irreducibly complex system creates a strong case for why transitional organisms are not found. That is because transitional forms would not be able to exist. If there were small steps from a fish becoming a land animal, the small transitional structure would not be able to work. For example, the transitions from gills to lungs in small minute steps would create systems that neither work for survival in water nor outside of water.

4.3.2 Flagellum

Furthermore, Behe found multiple aspects of the cell that seem to be irreducibly complex. The most controversial was the flagellum. Behe notes that the bacterial rotary motor of a flagellum must have the same mechanical elements as other rotary devices: a rotor (the rotating element) and a stator (the stationary component).[74] In addition, He states, "The bacterial flagellum is necessarily composed of at least three parts—a paddle, a rotor, and a motor—it is irreducibly complex. Gradual evolution of the flagellum, like the cilium, therefore, faces mammoth hurdles."[75] Furthermore, William Dembski coincides with Behe and makes the same argument.

Dembski says that from a Darwinian view, a bacterium with a flagellum evolved via the Darwinian selection mechanisms from a bacterium without a flagellum.[76] As Dembski elaborates,

> For this mechanism to produce the flagellum, chance modifications must generate the various proteins that constitute the flagellum. Then, selection must preserve them, gather them to the correct location in the bacterium, and adequately assemble them. Yet, how is a selection to accomplish this? Selection is nonteleological.

74. Behe, *Darwin's Black Box*, 67.
75. Behe, *Darwin's Black Box*, 68.
76. Dembski, *No Free Lunch*, 250.

Therefore, it cannot cumulate proteins, holding them in reserve until they are finally available to form a complete flagellum with the passing of many generations. The environment contains no blueprint of the flagellum that selection can extract and transmit to an organism to create a flagellum. Selection can only build on partial function, gradually improving existing function.[77]

Thus, it is impossible for a flagellum missing protein parts to function.[78]

These arguments for the flagellum created great controversy. Ian Musgrave gave a detailed response contrary to Behe and Dembski's view. He writes:

> Here is a possible scenario for the evolution of the eubacterial flagellum: a secretory system arose first, based around the SMC rod- and pore-forming complex, which was the common ancestor of the type-III secretory system and the flagellar system. The association of an ion pump (which later became the motor protein) to this structure improved secretion. Even today, the motor proteins, part of a family of secretion-driving proteins, can freely dissociate and reassociate with the flagellar design. The rod- and pore-forming complex may have rotated at this stage, as in some gliding-motility systems. The protoflagellar filament arose next as part of the protein-secretion structure (compare the Pseudomonas pilus, the Salmonella filamentous appendages, and the E. coli filamentous structures). Gliding-twitching motility arose at this stage or later and was then refined into swimming motility. Regulation and switching can be added later, because there are modern eubacteria that lack these attributes but function well in their environments (Shah and Sockett 1995). At every stage there is a benefit to the changes in the structure.[79]

---

77. Dembski, *No Free Lunch*, 250.
78. Dembski, *No Free Lunch*, 250.
79. Musgrave, "Evolution of the Bacterial Flagellum," 82–83.

The problem with Musgrave's statement is that it underestimates the complexity, variegation, diversity, of the flagellar system in its manufacturing apparatus and its "state-of-the-art design motif."[80] Jonathan McLatchie suggests that while there are dispensable components of flagella, it still remains that flagella has an irreducible core.[81]

4.3.3 Genetic Limits

4.3.3.1 Bacteria

A significant claim by a neo-Darwinist is that the mutations of bacteria in response to an antibiotic give a clear example of genetic mutations. Bacteria are indeed able to gain immunity from antibiotics. Therefore, one may conclude that genetic mutation on the macro-level is possible via natural selection. This was tested with the bacteria *Escherichia coli*. Hundreds of strains and varieties of *Escherichia coli* have been formed in experiments; however, they can still be easily identified as *Escherichia coli*. This is because a primitive nucleus was not created.[82]

These 1989 experiments have never produced a colony of bacterium with a primitive nucleus, and there has been no current observations in this manner.[83] There seems to be a genetic limit built into each basic type.[84] Zoologist and evolutionist Pierre-Paul Grasse comments on the bacteria study and says, "What is the use of their unceasing mutations if they do not change? In sum, the mutations of bacteria and viruses are merely *hereditary fluctuations* around a median position; a swing to the right, a swing to the left, *but not final evolutionary effect*" [Italics added].[85]

80. McLatchie, "Michael Behe."
81. Email correspondence with the author, Feb. 1, 2024.
82. Lester et al., *Natural Limits*, 88.
83. Lester et al., *Natural Limits*, 88.
84. Geisler and Turek, *Don't Have Enough Faith*, 142.
85. Grassé, *Evolution of Living Organisms*, 87.

4.3.3.2 Fruit Flies

One may object and say that it could eventually be observed with more time, but this was tried with the *Drosophila* fruit flies. These fruit flies are considered a "genetic workhorse" with a generation time of fewer than three weeks.[86] Within two years, thirty to forty generations can be observed in laboratory-controlled conditions.[87] These *Drosophila* are a definitive test for neo-Darwinian theory because they have been exposed to numerous mutations in a myriad of environments over periods covering many generations.[88] Ironically, despite the high degree of variability in *Drosophila*, they always remained to be fruit flies.[89] As Francis Hitchings says, "Fruit flies refuse to become anything but fruit flies under any circumstances yet devised."[90]

4.3.4 Cyclical Change

In addition to the genetic limits, the changing of species due to variability among life forms appears to be cyclical.[91] In 1835, Charles Darwin visited the Galapagos Islands and observed variations between finches due to the weather. His *On the Origin of Species* hinges on these variations. The problem is that these variations cycled back and forth depending on conditionings and appear to be limited to such a cycle. In all Darwin's observations, there was no observation of new life forms. In addition, these variations are of the utmost importance regarding Darwinian conclusions.

Darwin writes, "Individual differences are highly important for us, as they afford materials for natural selection to accumulate, in the same manner as man can accumulate in any given direction

---

86. Lester et al., *Natural Limits*, 88–89.
87. Lester et al., *Natural Limits*, 88–89.
88. Lester et al., *Natural Limits*, 88–89.
89. Lester et al., *Natural Limits*, 88–89.
90. Hitching, *Neck of the Giraffe*, 56–57.
91. Geisler and Turek, *Don't Have Enough Faith*, 144.

individual differences in his domesticated productions."[92] So, not only is there a cyclicality to these variations, but these variations would also have to be explained not only for the survival of species but the arrival of species.[93] The mechanism of natural selection does not offer this. It has no innovative capacity; it simply just eliminates or maintains what exists.[94]

One may object to say with more time, scientists would eventually see this micro to macro jump; however, there is no empirical evidence for this hypothesis. One can guess there might be a macro change, and it is fine to hold to that view. However, promoting it as an intractable fact would be intellectually dishonest. Notably, there seems to be evidence against this hypothesis as well.

4.4 Time and Chance
4.4.1 Cumulative Selection

Richard Dawkins argues that if you put a bunch of monkeys in a room with a twenty-six-letter typewriter, they would eventually be able to type the Shakespearean saying, "Methinks it is like a weasel."[95] With a single-step selection of random variation, the chance of getting the entire phrase of twenty-eight characters right with the twenty-seven letters of the phrase, "Methinks it is like a weasel," is 1/27 to the power 28, or, if you will, about 1 in 10,000 million million million million million million (10^{31}).[96] However, a cumulative selection would be much more effective.

With a computer generator, it can examine nonsense phrases and chooses the one which most resembles the target phrase, "Methinks it is like a weasel."[97] Richard Dawkins uses a computer to test this hypothesis and finds that within forty-three generations,

---

92. Darwin, *On the Origin*, 43.
93. Geisler and Turek, *Don't Have Enough Faith*, 144.
94. Müller, "Homology," 51.
95. Dawkins, *Blind Watchmaker*, 66.
96. Dawkins, *Blind Watchmaker*, 67.
97. Dawkins, *Blind Watchmaker*, 68.

the phrase, "Methinks it is like a weasel," can be generated.[98] So, instead of a chance of 10^{31}, it is only 43.[99] The problem with this is that this is not an unguided mindless process. Dawkins admits,

> If evolutionary progress had had to rely on single-step selection, it would never have got anywhere. If, however, there was any way in which the necessary conditions for cumulative selection could have been set up by the blind forces of nature, strange and wonderful might have been the consequences. Chance is a minor ingredient in the Darwinian recipe, but the most important ingredient is cumulative selection which is quintessentially nonrandom.[100]

Nevertheless, Dawkins has solved his own neo-Darwinian problem by introducing the two components that he explicitly wished to avoid at all costs.[101] If evolution is blind and purposeless, there cannot be a goal or target. This target phrase is the precise goal which, according to Dawkins, is un-Darwinian.[102] What is bizarre is that the information that the mechanisms are supposed to produce is already contained somewhere within the organism, whose genesis, Dawkins claims, to be simulated by this process.[103] No information would be generated without the target phrase.[104]

As Lennox notes, "The argument is entirely circular."[105] Additionally, if one genetic mistake is made, it will result in death. Dawkins also admits,

> The number of different ways of being dead is so much greater than the number of different ways of being alive, the chances are very high that a big random jump in genetic space will end in death... But the smaller the jump

---

98. Dawkins, *Blind Watchmaker*, 69.
99. Lennox, *God's Undertaker*, 167.
100. Dawkins, *Blind Watchmaker*, 70–71.
101. Lennox, *God's Undertaker*, 167.
102. Lennox, *God's Undertaker*, 167.
103. Lennox, *God's Undertaker*, 167.
104. Gitt, *In the Beginning*, 102.
105. Lennox, *God's Undertaker*, 167.

the less likely death is, and the more likely is it that the jump will result in improvement.[106]

The problem with this is genetic entropy.

As mentioned in chapter two, John C. Sanford discovered that genetic entropy is so strong within *large* genomes that selection cannot reverse it.[107] The higher the genome, the more compressed data.[108] This makes it extremely difficult, if not impossible, for smaller genetic jumps to happen for the higher genomes in humans. This is because mutations, more times than not, equal death. If one of Dawkins monkeys makes even one mistake, then the monkey dies.[109] Additionally, mutations are complex and happen at the molecular level, but not only that, selection can only happen on the level of the whole organism.[110] Due to this, it seems that the extinction of genomes is an inevitable pattern regardless of chance.[111]

4.4.2 DNA

The last resort would be to assume *a priori* that there is enough time in the history of life to make the neo-Darwinian paradigm plausible. One might argue, if the age of the earth is 4.5 billion years old, and life started about 3.8 billion years ago, there is bound to be enough time for life to form and evolve via randomized mutations. The main problem with this hypothesis is DNA.

DNA is a long molecule with a double helix structure consisting of four letters: A-C-G-T.[112] There is a rule that A is invariably paired with T and C with G; thus, if one strand of the double

---

106. Dawkins, *Blind Watchmaker*, 103.
107. Sanford, *Genetic Entropy*, 144.
108. Sanford, *Genetic Entropy*, 28.
109. Isaacs, "Interview."
110. Sanford, *Genetic Entropy*, 6.
111. Sanford, *Genetic Entropy*, 144.
112. Lennox, *God's Undertaker*, 136.

helix starts with AGGTCCGTAATG, then the other strand will start TCCAGGCATTAC.[113]

The importance of DNA is the sequencing. The sequencing of the letters of DNA is similar to the ordinary alphabet in that the message depends on the precise ordering of the letters; therefore, the sequence of bases on the spine of DNA carries a precise message.[114] A gene, then, is a long string of these letters carrying the information for a protein so that a gene can be interpreted as a set of instructions, like a program, for making that specific protein.[115]

In addition, there is an immense amount of DNA in even the simplest of lifeforms. Richard Dawkins acknowledges this tremendous quantity of information in life. He recalls that an amoeba contains as much information as a thousand Encyclopedia Britannicas.[116] With the complexity and quantity of DNA, it is appropriate to claim that DNA is vital for life due to the information and actions it carries out. This is where the problem of time and chance comes into play for the neo-Darwinist. The combinational probability for functional DNA mutations via a truly random, unguided, unintelligent process seems too small to base a scientific theory on.

4.4.3 Combinational Probability and the Chance Hypothesis

An amino acid chain contains twenty protein-forming amino acids. If a person has two amino acid chains, one will have 20^2 or 400 possible combinations of sequences.[117] However, it usually takes at least four amino acids for functional proteins and the genes (sections of the DNA that code for specific purposes)

---

113. Lennox, *God's Undertaker*, 136.
114. Lennox, *God's Undertaker*, 137.
115. Lennox, *God's Undertaker*, 137.
116. Dawkins, *Blind Watchmaker*, 164.
117. Meyer, *Darwin's Doubt*, 175.

consist of 1000 nucleotide bases at minimum.[118] When one takes the four letters of DNA (A,C,G,T) he or she now has 4^{1000} possible base sequences.[119] Additionally, it takes three bases to assign to one of the twenty protein-forming amino acids; so if the average gene minimum has 1000 bases, the average protein would have over 300 amino acids.[120]

This means that an average-length protein of 300 amino acids to form one possible sequence would be among 20^{300} or 10^{390} possible amino acid sequences.[121] To put this into perspective, there are only 10^{65} atoms estimated to be in the Milky Way galaxy.[122] Combinational-wise, this is an astronomical number of possible combinations. The trouble for a random, unguided, unintelligent process comes into play when looking at the rarity of functional DNA sequences. In addition, it depends if there is enough time to run all the possible sequencings to produce functions for life.

Douglas Axe set out to understand the probability of new genes and proteins emerging from nonfunctional genomes.[123] He used 150 amino acid long sequences that were capable of performing specific functions and compared them to the whole set of possible sequences according to the 150 amino acid length.[124] This is a very modest number of amino acid sequences. A simple Google search will even tell you that the average sequence length for bacteria is 320 amino acids. Regardless, Axe underwent mutagenesis experiments with the 150 amino acid long sequences and concluded that 10^{64} signature-consistent sequences form a working domain.[125] He then combined this with the prevalence of plausible

---

118. Meyer, *Darwin's Doubt*, 175.
119. Meyer, *Darwin's Doubt*, 175.
120. Meyer, *Darwin's Doubt*, 175.
121. Meyer, *Darwin's Doubt*, 175.
122. Meyer, *Darwin's Doubt*, 175.
123. Meyer, *Darwin's Doubt*, 198.
124. Axe, "Estimating the Prevalence," 1295–1315.
125. Axe, "Estimating the Prevalence," 1295.

hydropathic patterns and concluded that the overall prevalence of sequences performing a *specific function* is 10^{77}.[126]

This means that only one out of every 10^{77} sequences will result in a functional sequence for making one protein. This is much smaller than the total number of possible amino acid combinations; however, it is still an astronomically large number. Yet, the question again remains whether the probability is small enough to justify the neo-Darwinian model. It is important to also note that cells need to co-evolve with thousands of proteins at the same time which requires a living cell with DNA and proteins already functioning.

University of Georgia's Whitman et al. estimated that the number of prokaryotes that form each year amounts to approximately 10^{30}.[127] Michael Behe estimated that if this number had been the same over the history of life in the world (approximately 3.8 billion years), then there would have been slightly fewer than 10^{40} cells throughout the course of history.[128]

With this number and the prevalence of functioning sequences (10^{77}), one can calculate the conditional probability of generating a functioning gene sequence to be 1 in 10^{37} by dividing (10^{77}) / (10^{40}). This means if every single organism from the dawn of time was generated via random mutation, then one new base sequence in respect to the total space for all sequences would amount to only one sequence out of 10 trillion, trillion, trillion (10^{37}) sequences that need to be searched.[129]

In chance hypotheses, statisticians assess conditional probability by its probabilistic resources. Probabilistic resources "comprise the relevant ways an event can occur (replicational resources) and be specified (specificational resources) within a given context."[130] The vital question, therefore, is not "What is the probability of the event in question?" but rather, "What does its

126. Axe, "Estimating the Prevalence," 1295.
127. Whitman, Coleman, and Wiebe, "Prokaryotes," 6578.
128. Behe, *Edge of Evolution*, 59.
129. Meyer, *Darwin's Doubt*, 203.
130. Dembski, *Design Inference*, 181.

probability become after all the relevant probabilistic resources have been factored in?"[131] This is because probabilities must always be referred to a relevant class of probabilistic resources because they can never be considered in isolation.[132]

With this, if the conditional probability is less than ½ of the probabilistic resources, it is considered implausible.[133] As noted above, the conditional probability for genes mutating to create a specific function with the 10^{40} cells in the entire history of life equals a conditional probability of 1 in 10^{37}. This is immensely less than ½, which will, therefore, be considered implausible.

Additionally, the very complex information in DNA is not enough for the formation of animals. For animals to exist, a more complex type of information called epigenetic information is needed to form body parts. This includes the lifeforms found during the Cambrian period, which is dated around 350 million years ago.[134] Regardless of epigenetic information, the evidence for the origination of DNA from non-functional genomes is entirely implausible. Therefore, it is plausible to conclude that the *a priori* assumption of time and chance is unconvincing. When you add in epigenetic information, it just makes the case for neo-Darwinism more and more against the odds. As Richard Dawkins says, "We can accept a certain amount of luck in our explanations, but not too much."[135] Indeed, Dawkins is right.

4.5 Information and The Mind

A negative case was made concerning neo-Darwinism; however, one may postulate a positive case for an Intelligent Mind when looking at the nature information. This section will argue that all

---

131. Dembski, *Design Inference*, 181.
132. Dembski, *Design Inference*, 181.
133. Dembski, *Design Inference*, 181.
134. Müller and Newman, *Origination of Organismal Form*, 8.
135. Dawkins, *Blind Watchmaker*, 198.

life needs information, but the information itself cannot be material because it is dependent on a mind.

There are five levels to information: statistics, syntax, semantics, pragmatics, and apobetics. Statistics is the first level of information. It is composed of quantitative properties of languages that are dependent on frequencies.[136] It has nothing to do with its meaningfulness or sequencing of symbols.[137] In addition, grammatical correctness is excluded at this level.[138] Here is an example: Nxbq2394c5rytfinw3n79N&*^BF#*^&BFNSB#&^Ixe nr3im4ntvnmhy 80.

Syntax is the second level of information. This includes all structural properties of the process of setting up information.[139] The one interpreting it is only concerned with the actual sets of symbols (codes), and the rules governing how they are assembled into sequences (grammar and vocabulary) are independent of any meaning they may or may not have.[140] For example: Pigs the ball moon getting muskox the.

Semantics is the third level of information. The message can be conveyed by the conclusions and the meanings.[141] The sender and the recipient are interested in the meaning, which is based on the sequence of symbols into information.[142] At the semantic level, the purpose is the only invariant property, making it an essential information aspect.[143] For example:

The muskox is gallivanting along the icy tundra.

Pragmatics and apobetics are of the highest level of information. Pragmatics is information that has a request or command.[144] Here, the information can cause the recipient to take some action

136. Gitt, *In the Beginning*, 55.
137. Gitt, *In the Beginning*, 55.
138. Gitt, *In the Beginning*, 55.
139. Gitt, *In the Beginning*, 58.
140. Gitt, *In the Beginning*, 58.
141. Gitt, *In the Beginning*, 69.
142. Gitt, *In the Beginning*, 69.
143. Gitt, *In the Beginning*, 69.
144. Gitt, *In the Beginning*, 73.

(stimulate, initialize, or implement).[145] Gitt says, "This reactive functioning of information is valid for both inanimate systems (e. g., computers and an automatic car wash) as well as living organisms (e. g., activities in cells, actions of animals, and activities of human beings)."[146] An example of such can be seen in the following exhortation: Leave that muskox alone!

Apobetics is simply the completion of that pragmatic request. In the mentioned example above, the recipient of the information would, in fact, leave that muskox alone. The teleological aspect of this informational communication is essential because it concerns the premeditated purpose of the sender.[147]

The problem for neo-Darwinism now is the informational level of DNA. As noted in the preceding section, DNA is not random statistical information. Its message creates specific functions based on its order.[148] DNA is, in fact the highest level of information by requesting a certain function (pragmatics) and completing the action (apobetics). The dilemma for the neo-Darwinist is how to account for this information via natural causes in light of the empirical data of information. Information has always been observed and tested to have a mind behind it.

If a teacher writes the lesson plan with an expo marker on a whiteboard, the marker would be considered the material medium. Now, if the marker is wiped off, the total quantity of marker is still there; however, the information has vanished and has gone onto the eraser. The marker was a suitable material medium, but the essentiality was the arrangement of the particles of the marker. Moreover, this arrangement was not random because it had a mind (the teacher) behind it, ordering the sequences.

The following list contains empirical properties always postulated with information:

1. Information cannot exist without a code.

---

145. Gitt, *In the Beginning*, 75.
146. Gitt, *In the Beginning*, 75.
147. Gitt, *In the Beginning*, 75.
148. Lennox, *God's Undertaker*, 137.

2. Any code is the result of a free and deliberate convention.
3. There can be no information without a sender.
4. Any given chain of information points to a mental source.
5. There can be no information without volition (will).
6. There can be no information unless all five hierarchical levels are involved: statistics, syntax, semantics, pragmatics, and apobetics.
7. Information cannot originate in statistical processes.[149]

With this, one can conclude the following impossibilities:

1. It is impossible to set up, store, or transmit information without using a code.
2. It is impossible to have a code apart from a free and deliberate convention.
3. It is impossible that information can exist without having a mental source.
4. It is impossible for the information to exist without having been established voluntarily by free will.
5. It is impossible for the information to exist without all five hierarchical levels statistics, syntax, semantics, pragmatics, and apobetics.
6. It is impossible that information can originate in statistical processes.[150]

Now bringing this back to biology, one can now conclude the following about life:

1. Information is not life, but the information in cells is essential for all living beings.
2. Information is a necessary prerequisite for life.

---

149. Gitt, *In the Beginning*, 80.
150. Gitt, *In the Beginning*, 80.

3. Life is nonmaterial, and it is not information, but both entities—matter and information—are essential for life.
4. Information requires matter for storage and transmission.
5. Life requires information.
6. Biological life requires matter as a necessary medium.
7. Information and matter fall far short in describing life, but the life depends on the necessary conditions prevailing at the lower levels.[151]

Thus, the carriers of the information for life have been material, but the information itself is not material.[152]

When one looks at the information present in living organisms, the material could not be the genesis source because matter cannot be created or destroyed. So, when humans always, 10 times out of 10, postulate a mind behind information, why not postulate a mind behind the immense, and complex information found in DNA? One might appeal to "If we have more time, we'll find a natural cause;" however, this is appealing to a *Time of the Gaps* argument, which would be inappropriately assumed *a priori*.

In addition, if a theist appealed to the *God of the Gaps*, they also would be inappropriately assuming *a priori*. So, if one cannot assume *a priori* that unintelligent causes can produce information, how does one account for the genesis of the information in DNA (not the material medium)? Why is it then held among some scientists to seek a material cause of this information when researchers have never observed a material cause for information? If it cannot be material, then what is it? The following section will expound upon the presupposition of only accepting natural or material causes as plausible scientific causes.

---

151. Gitt, *In the Beginning*, 80.
152. Lennox, *God's Undertaker*, 178.

4.6 Methodological Naturalism

All the *a priori* assumptions for neo-Darwinism mentioned in this chapter hinge on the "big daddy" assumption of methodological naturalism. Methodological naturalism asserts that "to qualify as scientific, a theory must explain phenomena and events in nature—even events such as the origin of the universe and life or phenomena such as human consciousness—by reference to strictly material causes."[153] Methodological naturalism is a "ground rule" of science today, which requires scientists to seek explanations in the world around us based upon what scientists can observe, test, replicate, and verify.[154] Sandy Boucher categorizes methodological naturalism into intrinsic methodological naturalism and pragmatic naturalism.

According to intrinsic methodological naturalism, science by its very nature excludes supernatural explanations; it cannot postulate the supernatural without ceasing to be science.[155] Here, supernaturalist theories could be true, but they would not be considered science.[156] Pragmatic methodological naturalism allows no reason why science may not appeal to the supernatural. Boucher thinks that this is more of a guiding principle for science today, due to a poor "track record" of supernaturalist theories and explanations.[157] Any way one slices it, methodological naturalism suggests that only natural or material explanations should be considered scientific.

The problem with methodological naturalism is that it goes against the meaning of science. Science is and must be defined as an attempt to explain and understand the world people live in, epistemologically. As Norman Geisler and Frank Turek say, "Science is a search for causes."[158] The problem with holding to

153. Meyer, *Darwin's Doubt*, 383.
154. Lennox, *God's Undertaker*, 34.
155. Boucher, "Methodological Naturalism," 58.
156. Boucher, "Methodological Naturalism," 69.
157. Boucher, "Methodological Naturalism," 58.
158. Geisler and Turek, *Don't Have Enough Faith*, 120.

a strictly materialistic causal epistemology, is that it presupposes that materials can be the only cause. This is not only bad science but bad philosophy. The forensic nature of the science of the origin of life should be answered by "what caused the origin of life," not "what material cause caused the origin of life."

It is unwise and inappropriate to pigeonhole the cause of life to strictly material causes. This is because many scientific explanations depend on antecedent causal conditions and events, not laws, to do explanatory work;[159] if someone hits upon the wrong causes, then he has failed in the explanatory endeavor to discover the correct process one needs to employ to reach their conclusion.[160] This means that citing past causal events does more to explain a particular phenomenon than citing the existence of regularity in nature—simply because many things do not come in existence by a series of events that normally reoccur.[161]

The abnormal heights of the Himalayas are a prime example. A historical geologist who sets out to explain the cause of the height of the Himalayas will look for past causal events that were present in the Himalayan orogeny[162] but not in "normal height" orogenies.[163] Containing the knowledge of a general law that describes general orogeny will have little to no epistemic value in regard to the contrast of normal-height mountains and the Himalayas.[164] Instead, the geologist needs evidence of a specific set of past conditions.[165]

Sandy Boucher believes that there is nothing inherently unscientific about supernaturalist theories; however, he argues that there is no sufficient evidence in favor of supernatural theories.[166]

---

159. Meyer, "Laws, Causes, and Facts," 30.

160. Wilkenfeld and Lombrozo, "Inference to the Best," 1065.

161. Meyer, "Laws, Causes, and Facts," 30.

162. The process wherein part of the earth's crust is folded and reshaped by lateral compression, forming a mountain range.

163. Meyer, "Laws, Causes, and Facts," 30.

164. Meyer, "Laws, Causes, and Facts," 31.

165. Meyer, "Laws, Causes, and Facts," 31.

166. Boucher, "Methodological Naturalism," 58.

He concedes that inferences to intelligent design are intelligible and could potentially count as scientific; however, he argues that the inference to supernatural or divine intelligent design cannot be considered scientific because scientists cannot attach a sense to the notion of the supernatural.[167]

This sidesteps something that humans can innately know and understand. The supernatural can be connotatively defined and "made sense" off. Boucher is guilty of his prior commitment to materialism while making this claim. He is assuming materialism *a priori* to "attach no sense" to the supernatural.[168] The supernatural is that which supersedes the laws of nature. People know the laws of nature by their repeatability and testability. Indeed, one cannot prove them within 100 percent of certainty; however, one has to come to an empirical conclusion, eventually.

If one continues to see causal instances in nature that seem not to have a natural or material cause, then there needs to eventually be a concession. Time and chance are not appropriate or convincing assumptions in which to place one's faith. Like information, if humans constantly postulate a mind behind information since the beginning of human consciousness, one can see that information is not material or caused by the material. So, the cause must supercede nature, making it *super*natural.

In this case, it would be agency. As Meyer says, "Agency is much more appropriate in causal history. Forensic science, history, and archeology all sometimes postulate the past activity of human agents to account for the emergence of particular objects or events."[169]

The deeper problem is that methodological naturalism seems to be an *a priori* assumption based plainly on an unsupported dogmatic faith. It is certain when one inquires about Richard Lewontin's statement:

---

167. Boucher, "Methodological Naturalism," 71.

168. This debate requires a much deeper discussion regarding the controversial topic of miracles and goes beyond the scope of this book.

169. Meyer, "Laws, Causes, Facts," 33.

We take the side of science in spite of the patent absurdity of some of its constructs, in spite of its failure to fulfill many of its extravagant promises of health and life, in spite of the tolerance of the scientific community for unsubstantiated just-so stories, because we have a prior commitment, a commitment to materialism. It is not that the methods and institutions of science somehow compel us to accept a material explanation of the phenomenal world, but, on the contrary, that we are forced by our *a priori* adherence to material causes to create an apparatus of investigation and a set of concepts that produce material explanations, no matter how counter-intuitive, no matter how mystifying to the uninitiated. Moreover, that materialism is absolute, for we cannot allow a Divine Foot in the door.[170]

This seems to be the real problem. Allowing a "Divine Foot" in the door of science may have crucial implications outside the realm of science. It may be why certain *ad hoc hypotheses* are held onto despite the ample evidence against them. The question to now ponder is if this bias is in the world of science, and if so, why?

4.7 Biases for Darwinian Theory

It seems like Richard Dawkins gives a "bye" to Darwinian theory by saying that it requires some imagination. He says, "It took a very large leap of the imagination for Darwin and Alfred Wallace to see that, contrary to all intuition, there is another way and, once you have understood it, a far more plausible way, for complex 'design' to arise out of primeval simplicity."[171] David Berlinski notes that Wallace identified a direct conflict between his theory and what seemed to him apparent facts about the solidity and unchangeability of human nature.[172] It is evident when one reads what Wallace once said:

---

170. Lewontin, "Billions and Billions."
171. Dawkins, *Blind Watchmaker*, preface.
172. Berlinski, *Devil's Delusion*, 159.

> Certain purely physical characteristics of the human race are not explicable on the theory of variation and survival of the fittest. The brain, the organs of speech, the hand, and the external form of man, offer some special difficulties in this respect, to which we will briefly direct attention.[173]

In Western civilization, around the 1600s to 1800s, a rise in secularism occurred within politics.[174] There are several reasons for this, but the advancement of empirical science, the decline of religious belief, and the interweaving of sociology with evolutionary explanations have been prominent antecedent causes.[175] Society reached a humanistic point where evolutionary developments influenced all aspects of the human experience.[176] The study of human evolution has been and remained as much a prescriptive enterprise as a descriptive one.[177]

In addition, people have appealed to biological evolution as a means of justification for a range of political views since the publications of the evolutionary ideas of Étienne Geoffroy Saint-Hilaire and Jean-Baptiste Lamarck.[178] Moreover, Robert Chamber's *Vestiges of Natural History of Creation* published anonymously in 1844, is widely noted to have "prepared the soil" for the acceptance of Darwin's *Origin of Species* in 1859.

Notice an interesting passage from the book:

> We know the historical era to only a tiny portion of the entire age of our globe. We do not know what may have happened during the ages which preceded its commencement, as we do not know what may happen in ages yet in the distant future. Therefore, we can properly infer from the apparently invariable production of like by like that such is the ordinary procedure of nature in

---

173. Wallace, "Sir Charles Lyell," 391.
174. Rubens, *Politics and Neo-Darwinism*, chapter one.
175. Rubens, *Politics and Neo-Darwinism*, chapter one.
176. Hale, *Political Descent*, 2.
177. Hale, *Political Descent*, 3.
178. Hale, *Political Descent*, 7.

the time immediately passing before our eyes. Mr. Babbage's illustration shows how this ordinary procedure may be subordinate to a higher law that interrupts and changes it in proper season.[179]

Materialists, atheists, radicals, and revolutionaries adduced to this theme of progressive naturalism to support their political and societal endeavors.[180] One can see this in a quote by Karl Marx: "I have read all manner of things. Inter alia, Darwin's book on Natural Selection. Although developed in the crude English fashion, this is the book which, in the field of natural history, provides the basis for our views."[181]

In addition, if the proposition of Darwinism can give intellectual justification for atheism, it may rid the moral accountability that major religions push. If atheism is true, people can do whatever they want because they have no higher being to give account to. It sounds like a far stretch; however, as noted in the literature review, Julian Huxley was once asked on television why evolution was accepted so quickly. He said, "The reason we accepted Darwinism even without proof is that we didn't want God to interfere with our sexual mores."[182] This is a mind-blowing statement because the modern neo-Darwinian paradigm has pontificated throughout the world as an intractable fact.

Moreover, if the neo-Darwinian paradigm were wrong, neo-Darwinists would surrender authority regarding the truth because the public views them as revered authority figures.[183] Allowing the possibility of God to relinquish their claim of superior authority would be admitting that they do not have absolute authority when explaining causes.[184] If God exists, they could not explain everything due to predictable natural laws.[185] Richard

179. Chambers, *Vestiges of the Natural History*, 219.
180. Hale, *Political Descent*, 12.
181. Marx and Engels, *Collected Works*, 231.
182. Huxley, *Skeptics Answered*, epilogue.
183. Geisler and Turek, *Don't Have Enough Faith*, 162.
184. Geisler and Turek, *Don't Have Enough Faith*, 162.
185. Geisler and Turek, *Don't Have Enough Faith*, 162.

THE BLIND SCIENTIST

Lewontin put it this way: "To appeal to an omnipotent deity is to allow that at any moment the regularities of nature may be ruptured, that miracles may happen."[186] So, insecurity about the unknowable may be a reason.

Instead, a more likely reason for holding to neo-Darwinism for many scientists could be financial stability. There is enormous pressure in academia to publish research that furthers the neo-Darwinian paradigm.[187] If these scientists and professors stop doing research in this manner, they may quickly be out of a job. If they have a family to support, it only adds to the reluctance, understandably.

These reasons may collectively be why there is so much emotion behind it. Notice Richard Dawkins' famous remark in a book review, "It is absolutely safe to say that if you meet somebody who claims not to believe in evolution, that person is ignorant, stupid or insane (or wicked, but I'd rather not consider that)."[188]

In addition, notice the sarcasm in David Prindle concerning God and evolution:

> God might have shepherded evolution along a course he had planned out ahead of time. He also might have created the natural laws, then sat back to watch them work themselves out over 3.8 billion years of the history of life. Or, he might have created the natural laws, watched life struggle at the limits of single-cell existence for 3.2 billion years, then gotten bored and intervened, just once, to push life over the threshold into multicellular splendor. Or, he might have created the universe and its natural laws 13.7 billion years ago, then gotten distracted by his model train collection and lost track of time for 13 billion years, after which he looked up and was startled to discover that life had sprung up, according to those laws, without any further help. Or, he might have created the universe and its natural laws, watched the whole system work itself out, including the evolution of unicellular

---

186. Lewontin, "Billions and Billions of Demons."
187. Geisler and Turek, *Don't Have Enough Faith*, 162.
188. Dawkins, "In Short."

to multicellular life, and finally decided, about 200,000 years ago, to intervene and create Homo sapiens.[189]

Before ending this section, it is essential to note that biases do not mean that certain propositions are not true. One may have undue bias against either Intelligent Design or neo-Darwinism and be in an entirely ignorant epistemic standing, but it does not affect the raw data. It may, however, affect how one interprets such evidence, as what was shown in this chapter.

4.8 Final Thoughts

This chapter has covered the evidence for the five *a priori* assumptions necessary for neo-Darwinian conclusions (gradualism, the tree of life hypothesis, the micro to macro-evolutionary jump, time and chance, and methodological naturalism) and demonstrated how each of these assumptions do not rest on a scientific interpretative method but rely on ad hoc assumptions that seem to be rooted in the want to eliminate the intellectual need for theistic postulations. First, the relationship between *a priori* assumptions and science was expanded to create a greater understanding of what is appropriate and not appropriate when assuming something in scientific study.

It was then demonstrated that the evidence of the "Cambrian Explosion" seems to strongly contradict the *a priori* assumptions of gradualism and the tree of life hypothesis. Complex life seems to have appeared in one massive influx rather than small gradualistic steps over a long period of time. Assumptions like Gould's punctuated equilibrium are instilled to cover up the contracting evidence, but there is no independent evidence for this theory. The assumption was changed, and no new data was found. This is *ad hoc* and inappropriate to be considered scientific fact.

The evidence for micro-evolution was then shown that it could not undoubtedly account for the macro-evolutionary model. Genetic limits, cyclical change, and irreducible complexity can all be observed empirically to show that there are limits

189. Prindle, *Politics of Evolution*, 82–83.

within life that seem to hinder large evolutionary jumps. Even if one grants 3.8 billion years of life to exist on Earth, more time is needed to account for the complex life people see today to evolve via random genetic mutations. It was demonstrated that there is a 1 in 10^{37} chance that DNA sequences can be arranged to form life-functioning sequences from very short 150-long amino acid chains. In probability theory, this is equal to a zero percent chance for life evolving via chance.

The level of information found in DNA is among the highest and most complex information (pragmatics and apobetics), making it reasonable in postulating an intelligent mind behind the information in DNA. So, if the information is not material but necessary for life, then something immaterial can be the necessary cause for life. This postulation of intelligence as a casual indicator for information has often been observed.

It was then shown that this faith is grounded in a materialist scientific methodology. Suppose life relies on immaterial means, and those immaterial means seem best postulated from some sort of causal intelligence. In that case, it is only fitting to conclude that the mind is responsible for all life seen today rather than an unguided random process. Yet, it was shown that strong biases are placed in the minds of neo-Darwinist, even to the point of admitting that they cannot allow a "Divine Foot" in the door to fight against the Intelligent Design hypothesis. This may be the cause for the ad hoc explanations to cover up the contradicting evidence of the neo-Darwinian paradigm. Overall, this chapter demonstrated that the *a priori* assumptions necessary for neo-Darwinian conclusion seem to be unsupported, unconvincing, and individually biased.

5

Neo-Darwinism and Christian Apologetics

MANY NEO-DARWINISTS ACCUSE CHRISTIANS of relying blindly on faith and erroneous presuppositions to justify their beliefs. This chapter will illuminate the epistemology behind the three apologetic methods (presuppositionalism, evidentialism, and experientialism) that a Christian can use to justify their belief in God and then synthesize how neo-Darwinism would theoretically fit into each apologetic method.

The prior chapter showed how neo-Darwinian *a priori* assumptions (presuppositions) are not based on an evidential epistemology, and it will now be shown how neo-Darwinism is, in fact, much more presuppositional in its methodology because of its appeal to experientialism. This will then demonstrate how the epistemology behind neo-Darwinism affects its methodology because "epistemology modifies methodology and justifies the knowledge produced."[1]

---

1. Carter and Little, "Justifying Knowledge," 1317.

5.1 Christian Apologetics

Apologetics comes from the Greek word, ἀπολογία (apologia), which means to give a defense. This is demonstrated in 1 Peter 3:15 (ESV), where Peter is writing to other Christians on how to endure persecution for their faith in Christ. In the passage, Peter says, "But in your hearts honor Christ the Lord as holy, always being prepared to make a *defense* to anyone who asks you for a reason for the hope that is in you; yet do it with gentleness and respect."

A satisfactory modern definition of Christian apologetics would be an intellectual defense for the truthfulness of Christianity. The method of one's defense can be contingent on a variety of theological and philosophical positions—hence, the reason for relating neo-Darwinian theory to apologetical methods. Epistemology plays a crucial role in one's interpreting methods and methodology.

5.2 Presuppositionalism

The presuppositional apologetic method has been greatly pioneered by apologists Cornelius Van Til and Greg Bahsen. It can be recapitulated by three main points:

1. There is no neutral starting point between the Christian and non-Christian. Therefore, one must presuppose either.
2. Consequently, Christians should presuppose Christianity in their apologetic method and seek to show how only upon Christian presuppositions can one make sense of reality.
3. The transcendental argument: Only if God exists can there be a basis for morality, science, history, and rationality.[2]

Van Til argued that "God's being and knowledge are absolutely comprehensive; such knowledge is too wonderful for man, he cannot attain it."[3] For Van Til, once someone decides to utilize

---

2. Wartick, "Presuppositional Apologetic."
3. Van Til, *Defense of the Faith*, 28.

evidential arguments outside of Christianity, they have granted the non-believer's presuppositions and are therefore doomed to fail.[4] Greg Bahnsen says something very similar.

He notes that the apologist must demonstrate that without a Christian presupposition, there can be no intelligible use of facts and logic.[5] Without this presupposition, he believes "Human knowledge and interpretation fail instantly."[6] Because of this rationale, Bahnsen believes "to be reasonable at all, men must submit to the ultimate standard of God's self-attesting word; to refuse this is to insist upon intellectual foolishness and eternal damnation."[7]

This type of apologetical method is held mostly by reformed theology camps like James R. White and Doug Wilson. However, there are reformed theologians (such as R.C. Sproul) who hold to a more evidential approach, which will be discussed in the next section.

The epistemology of this apologetical method does not make Christianity the conclusion of an argument; rather, it makes Christianity the starting presupposition.[8] This is similar to neo-Darwinian theory. As mentioned in the prior chapter, for example, they start with the presupposition of a tree of life and use that presupposition to shape the way the data is interpreted to arrive at the conclusion for a tree of life. In this case, there is limited supporting evidence for the tree of life, and yet it is presupposed to be true.

5.3 Evidentialism

Christian evidentialist favor positive evidence for the veridicality of Christianity. There are two camps of this methodology: classical and evidential. The primary difference between these two is not their epistemology but their methodology.

4. Wartick, "Presuppositional Apologetic."
5. Bahnsen, *Presuppositional Apologetics*, 14.
6. Bahnsen, *Presuppositional Apologetics*, 14.
7. Bahnsen, *Presuppositional Apologetics*, 14.
8. Wartick, "Presuppositional Apologetic."

5.3.1 Classical Apologetics

Classical apologists are prospective in their line of reasoning. They utilize a two-step method wherein they start with reasons and arguments for God's existence (natural theology), and then work their way up to Christian evidences for Jesus Christ.[9] The classical method resembles Thomas Aquinas' Five Ways[10] of demonstrating God's existence in his *Summa Theologica* in addition to his appeal to the signs of credibility (miracles and prophecy) to validate Christian doctrine.[11] Additionally, the "father of modern apologetics,"[12] Hugo Grotius, utilized the traditional methodology of arguments of natural theology and inaugurated a historical approach to the truth of Gospels in his *De Veritate Religionis Christianae*.[13]

5.3.2 Evidential Apologetics

The name may cause some confusion, but this is simply a methodological distinction. Different from classical apologetics, evidential apologetics have a one-step approach wherein they treat one or more historical arguments for the resurrection of Christ as being able both to indicate God's existence and activity and to indicate which variety of theism is true.[14] Well-known historian and evidentialist Gary Habermas notes, "Evidentialist and classical apologists have much in common, with the major distinction being the use of historical evidence."[15] So, instead of a prospective method (bottom-up), evidentialists use a retrospective (top-down)

---

9. Craig, "Classical Apologetics," 28.
10. Kenny, *Five Ways*, 1.
11. Craig, "Classical Apologetics," 28.
12. Gundry and Cowan, *Five Views*, 22.
13. Craig, "Classical Apologetics," 28.
14. Habermas, "Evidential Apologetics," 92.
15. Habermas, "Evidential Apologetics," 92.

method by arguing for miracles through the resurrection of Jesus Christ and then working their way down to belief in God.

5.3.3 Differentiating Between Evidential Epistemology and Apologetic Method

Habermas notes that this apologetic method should be distinct from evidential epistemology. Evidential epistemology occurs when one's beliefs are guided and/or constrained by evidence. Here, "Person S is justified in believing proposition p at time t if and only if S's evidence for p at t supports believing."[16] This can be bifurcated into two categories: strict and moderate evidentialism.

Strict evidentialism is based on the work of William Kingdon Clifford, known as the *Clifford Principle*. The Clifford Principle states, "It is wrong always, everywhere and for anyone, to believe anything upon insufficient evidence."[17] Many non-Christian evidentialists (such as Clifford, John Locke, and David Hume) add the condition that the amount of evidence in one's possession must be proportionate to the degree of one's belief, therefore, one should only firmly believe something on the basis of sufficient evidence (where "sufficient" involves the evidence being strong enough for the belief to count as knowledge if true).[18]

Moderate evidentialists take the principles of strict evidentialism and allow some circumstances in which subjects are rationally permitted to form beliefs in the absence of sufficient evidence; however, if the number of exceptions is very large, then the position ends up looking more like a non-evidentialist position.[19] Gary Habermas notes that evidential epistemology holds that beliefs are justified only if one has conclusive evidence for them. The apologetic strategy says that there are good arguments for Christian theism, but that there is not much to say concerning

---

16. Mittag, "Evidentialism."
17. Clifford, "Ethics of Belief," 118.
18. Clifford, "Ethics of Belief."
19. Chignell, "Ethics of Belief."

the type or amount of evidence, or just how much argumentation is necessary to justify a belief.[20]

From a theological perspective, some evidentialists suggest that the Holy Spirit can provide direct and sufficient confirmation to the individual concerning the truth of Christianity apart from any evidence.[21] Hence, more than one epistemic stance could encourage the use of some form of evidential apologetic methodology.[22]

5.3.4 Neo-Darwinism and Evidentialism

From a methodological and epistemological standpoint, neo-Darwinian theory violates both. The last chapter demonstrated how all the *a priori* assumptions necessary for neo-Darwinian conclusion are unsupported, unconvincing, and unscientific. An epistemological perspective strongly shows how neo-Darwinian theory is not evidential. There is limited empirical evidence for macro-evolutionary change; therefore, strict evidentialism is out. Neo-Dariwinism may be closer to moderate evidentialism; however, if this means is used, neo-Darwinism would allow too many expectations to justify people's epistemic positions.

There is a disproportionate amount of guessing for neo-Darwinism to be considered moderately evidential—especially when moderate evidentialists hold to Cliffordian principles when considering impactful beliefs.[23] For example:

> beliefs formed by a military pilot about the location of a legitimate bombing target amid a residential area, or the beliefs formed by a government health official regarding the efficacy of a pharmaceutical trial, at least insofar as these beliefs lead to morally or prudentially significant actions are impactful beliefs where *much is at stake*. But at the same time, they might think it

20. Habermas, "Evidential Apologetics," 92–93.
21. Habermas, "Evidential Apologetics," 93.
22. Habermas, "Evidential Apologetics," 94.
23. Chignell, "Ethics of Belief."

permissible to abandon these strict standards in ordinary contexts where *not much is at stake*—for instance, the everyday belief that there is still some milk in the fridge. [Italics added][24]

From a Christian evidential apologetic standpoint, neo-Darwinism also lacks credulity because the methodology of both classical and evidential apologetics is based on drawing inferences to the best explanation. Neo-Darwinian theory (as a whole) does not do that. Stephen Jay Gould's punctuated equilibrium attempts to draw a better inference than gradualism, and it does seem to be a better position; however, its position is circular because it assumes punctuation rather than drawing inferences from empirical data. Additionally, the use of the evidence for micro-evolution and accounting it as macro-evolution has no inference to the best explanation because there has never been an observation of macro-evolutionary change (in addition to the absence of transitional forms in the fossil record).

Furthermore, when looking at probability theory and the chances of life arriving from non-life, neo-Darwinism defies a moderate evidentialist position because the level of impact that neo-Darwinism has as a worldview is far too high to justify the 1 out of 10^{37} chance of life forming from non-life. The ideological reinforcements of neo-Darwinism in social structures like the public school system, academic culture, and the media in Western civilization make the stakes much too high to consider neo-Darwinism evidential when utilizing epistemological evidentialism's own definition.[25]

5.4 Experientialism

Experientialism is when experience is the source of knowledge. Experiential apologetics claims that all truth is determined by experience and that there is a recognizable and self-attesting religious

---

24. Chignell, "Ethics of Belief."
25. McGrath, *Darwinism and the Divine*, 35.

experience.[26] Clifford Williams makes an experiential apologetic based on needs. One thing to note about Clifford's experientialism is that need with reason is blind, but reason without need is sterile.[27] William's argument follows:

1. We need cosmic security. We need to know that we will live beyond the grave in a state that is free from the defects of this life, a state that is full of goodness and justice. We need a more expansive life, one in which we love and are loved. We need meaning, and we need to know that we are forgiven for going astray. We also need to experience awe, to delight in goodness and to be present with those we love.
2. Faith in God satisfies these needs.
3. Therefore, we are justified in having faith in God.[28]

This argument is not pessimistic like the ones of existentialist writers Albert Camus and Jean-Paul Sartre.[29] Their particular brand of existentialism swirls around the darker facets of the human personality, which in return does not lead them into a faith in God.[30] Williams's experiential argument is much more fitting to the existentialism of Søren Kierkegaard, also known as the father of existentialism. However, Kierkegaard is similar to Camus and Sartre by probing the deep recess of the mind, but he ends up with a completely different conclusion by uncovering subtle ways people hide from God and then entices the reader out of hiding from God.[31]

---

26. Geisler, *Christian Apologetics*, 70.
27. Williams, *Existential Reasons*, 12.
28. Williams, *Existential Reasons*, 32.
29. Williams, *Existential Reasons*, 32.
30. Williams, *Existential Reasons*, 32.
31. Williams, *Existential Reasons*, 32.

5.5 Where Does Neo-Darwinism Fall?

Experientially, neo-Darwinism appeals to the existentialism of Fredrich Nietzsche, Albert Camus, and John Paul Sartre. The pessimistic existentialism makes man the ultimate voice of reason in determining one's own will. This can be seen when reading Julian Huxley: "Evolution helps us to understand ourselves as unique organisms equipped with a new 'method of evolution'—cultural evolution—based on the cumulative transmission of experience through language and symbols."[32] Huxley says this new organization of thought, belief system, framework of values, or ideology, must grow and be developed in the light of the new evolutionary vision.[33]

With this appeal, the neo-Darwinist acquires certain presuppositions that take God out of the equation and uses these presuppositions to shape the way data is interpreted. If humanity does not need God for a framework of values, then it is easy to see why the neo-Darwinist does not see the need to conclude an Intelligent Designer (God) in his or her scientific studies. This may sound far-fetched but consider Richard Dawkins's speculative statement in an interview with Ben Stein in the context of how the origin of life happened:

> It (the origin of life) could come about some earlier time in the universe. Some civilizations evolved by probably some Darwinian means to a very higher level of technology and designed a form of life that they seeded onto perhaps this planet . . . You might find evidence for that when you look at the detail of biochemistry and molecular biology. You might find a signature of some designer. And that designer could well be a higher intelligence from elsewhere in the universe, but that higher intelligence would itself have to come about by some explicable process.[34]

---

32. Huxley, *Essays of a Humanist*, 127.
33. Huxley, *Essays of a Humanist*, 83.
34. Dawkins, *Expelled*.

THE BLIND SCIENTIST

As Ben Stein notes, "So, Dawkins is not against Intelligent Design just certain types of designers such as God."[35] Aliens that seeded life on this planet are a perfectly fine and intriguing hypothesis, but somehow the notion of a superterrestrial deity is not.

In 1859, Charles Darwin did not write a book called, "The Small Changes in Species," but *On the Origin of Species*. The observations of Darwin cannot evidentially support the origin of species. So, why call it that? Dawkins even admits that when it comes to the cause of the origin of life, he replies, "Nobody knows how it started."[36] If nobody knows how the origin of all life started, and if one could find a signature of some designer with higher intelligence and/or capabilities, then why be so rigid about not allowing the possibility of God being that designer?

If Dawkins and other neo-Darwinists' presuppositions are unprovable yet so strongly directed, then their promotion must be about something else. As John Lennox says,

> If you have two distinguished scientists and the fact that you can range many more on each side you know, saying exactly the opposite things; that's telling me that the conflict is not between science and belief in God; otherwise, you'd expect all scientists to be atheists. But it's worldview conflict. It is between scientists who have different worldviews.[37]

Indeed, this seems to be the case, especially concerning the presuppositions that Christians and non-Christians have when conducting science. Christians presuppose that intelligence comes from intelligence, design comes from a designer, everything has a cause, and that God is the causal Creator for all creation. Not surprisingly, Christians use this worldview and come to different conclusions than neo-Darwinists. So, it is not necessarily the facts that Christians and neo-Darwinists argue over, but the circumstances and forces surrounding the facts.

One could easily ask if it would be possible for both sides to agree to disagree and be on their way. Yet, such a *détente* is

---

35. Stein, *Expelled*.
36. Dawkins, *Expelled*.
37. Lennox, *Expelled*.

not allowed by current neo-Darwinist scientific leaders, apparently. Scientific naturalism leads to a far different place with far different priorities and prohibitions (or a lack thereof) than does Christianity. Yet, the ramifications of the wrong conclusions and methods—for both worldviews—has and will lead to unpleasant consequences when acted out, improperly.

For instance, many skeptics have problems with Christianity because of church history controversies such as the Inquisition and the Crusades, but those dark periods do not accurately reflect the teachings of Jesus in the Bible. Jesus taught his followers to love their enemies (Matt 5:43–46 ESV), and He displayed this personally by enduring a sacrificial death to vicariously take on the curse of God for the sake of all humanity (Heb 9:11–12, ESV). Likewise, one does not blame Bach or Beethoven for a sixth-grade band's terrible performance. Bach and Beethoven's musical compositions are sublime; however, they only sound as good as the musicians performing that day.

Conversely, if neo-Darwinism has been poorly composed, then one would not or could not expect scientists to embrace or promote such an inferior work. As historian Mark Cartwright has noted regarding the astronomical difficulties embedded in the Ptolemaic model of the planets (which inevitably ended mathematically in a celestial collision without artificial manipulation), "Copernicus knew of and studied all of these theories, but their complexity seemed contrived to explain an original model that was perhaps itself flawed. Change the central equant point and perhaps the physical behaviour of the planets would become clearer, and the theory that explained it a whole lot simpler."[38]

Good science requires reasonable, straightforward theories than rest upon their own merits without duplicity, pretense, or contrivance to maintain their functionality. Based on the aforementioned scrutinization, neo-Darwinism fails to meet the traditional standards of balanced scientific methodology. The question naturally follows, then, on what can and should be done to solve this dilemma, which will be discussed in the final chapter.

38. Cartwright, "Nicolaus Copernicus."

6

Implications, Discussions, and Solutions for Neo-Darwinian Limitations

IT WAS SHOWN THROUGHOUT this book that the *a priori* assumptions necessary for neo-Darwinian conclusions are unsupported, unconvincing, and individually biased. Generally, neo-Darwinism is defined as life evolving to its present state of complexity and diversity via a purposeless material mechanism of random genetic change and natural selection.[1] It has been demonstrated that there is significant contention among scientists and philosophers regarding the efficacy of the *a priori* assumptions necessary for these neo-Darwinian conclusions.

Critics will claim that religious precursors are the reasons for the pushback of neo-Darwinism. However, there is a variety of different scientists and philosophers with different worldviews that see an issue with neo-Darwinism's *a priori* assumptions. Christians like John Lennox, Stephen Myer, Francis Collins, Alister McGrath, William Dembski, Michael Behe, Werner Gitt, Norman Geisler, Alvin Plantinga, and the like are several who see significant

1. Johnson, "Introduction," 1–3.

problems with neo-Darwinism. However, some distinct theological differences exist within particular scholarly Christian camps. For example, Francis Collins and Alister McGrath are theistic-evolutionists and Michael Behe is a Catholic.

Additionally, it is not only Christians that see the issue with neo-Darwinism's *a priori* assumptions. Secular Jew David Berlinski has been a heavyweight in contesting neo-Darwinism. Furthermore, it was shown that atheist Thomas Nagel also found massive problems with neo-Darwinism. Not only that, secular scientists such as Christian Schwabe, Gerd Müller, Stuart Newman, Patt Willmer, and Simon Conway Morris all found morphological issues with neo-Darwinism based on the evidence left by the Cambrian explosion.

Interestingly enough, atheistic scholars Richard Dawkins, Michael Ruse, Ernst Mayr, Julian Huxley, Stephen Jay Gould, Richard Lewontin, and Sandy Boucher presume that neo-Darwinism is more or less a fact and that their *a priori* assumptions are adequate. Note that it has been clarified that not all *a priori* assumptions are flawed. For instance, the laws of logic and the laws of nature must be assumed *a priori* to do good science. Additionally, the qualitative nature of most sciences—in this context, biology—must heavily rely on *a priori* assumptions. However, neo-Darwinism's *a priori* assumptions—gradualism, the tree of life hypothesis, the evidence of micro-evolution accounting for macro-evolutionary change, time and chance, and the big-daddy assumption, methodological naturalism—all seem to be unsupported, unconvincing, and individually biased.

The evidence unaccounted for in the Cambrian explosion, the gap of non-existing evidence between the evidence for micro-evolution and macro-evolution, irreducibly complex systems like the flagellum, the genetic limits and cyclical change within species, the 1 in 10^{37} chance of DNA producing life requiring functions, and the empirical evidence of information and the mind, all seem to contradict the *a priori* assumptions a neo-Darwinist needs to maintain neo-Darwinian conclusions adequately.

Consequently, it was also shown that there might be more profound reasons for holding on to neo-Darwinist beliefs. It seems that many Neo-Darwinists have a cognitive dissonance with the evidence and their conclusions. Richard Lewontin is an example of this. To bring up his stance one more time, he believes we should force an *a priori* adherence to material causes no matter how counter-intuitive it may seem so that we do not allow a "Divine Foot" in the door.[2]

This seems to be the underlying aspiration. Neo-Darwinists do not want God to exist. This was clearly shown in the previous chapter where Richard Dawkins indicated that he was okay with an intelligent designer—as long as it is not God. To bring up his ad hoc statement again, Dawkins thinks it is plausible that perhaps aliens of higher intelligence seeded the planet because of the signature of some designer found in DNA.[3] Yet, he is not okay with God being this Intelligent Designer.

With everything considered, it may be plausible to conclude that neo-Darwinists do not want God to exist. So, they try (despite the evidence) to show that science can disprove God, but it seems that no matter how hard they strive to bury God with scientific aphorisms, some skeptics break this dissonance and suggest the evidence shows that a god may exist. This happened to the most notorious atheist against theism—Antony Flew.

Near the end of Flew's life, he gave up his atheistic belief. Coincidentally, it was the evidence from DNA that had a significant influence on his change of mind. Consider what he said in his book, *There is a God: How to World's Most Notorious Atheist Changed His Mind*:

> When asked if recent work on the origin of life pointed to the activity of a creative Intelligence, I said: Yes, I now think it does . . . almost entirely because of the DNA investigations. What I think DNA material has done is that it has shown, by the almost unbelievable complexity of the arrangements which are needed to produce (life),

2. Lewontin, "Billions and Billions."
3. Dawkins, *Expelled.*

that intelligence must have been involved in getting these extraordinarily diverse elements to work together. It's the enormous complexity of the number of elements and the enormous subtlety of the ways they work together. The meeting of these two parts at the right time by chance is simply minute. It is all a matter of the enormous complexity by which the results were achieved, which looked to me like the *work of intelligence*.[4]

This is interesting, to say the least. The postulations of information coming from a mind play a crucial role in Flew's change of mind (no pun intended). Yet, John Lennox points out that this idea of information and the mind has been going on for centuries. In the Bible, John 1:1 states, "In the beginning was the Word, and the Word was with God, and the Word was God. He was in the beginning with God. *All things were made through him, and without him was not anything made that was made.*"

The Greek for "Word" is λόγος (logos), which is a term that Stoic philosophers use for the rational principle behind the universe which conveys massive implications of command, meaning, code, and communication—i.e., information.[5] The *Word* is much more fundamental than mass and energy because they both belong to the category of the created,[6] but the *Word* does not.[7] The point to be driven home is that "The Creator of the Universe is this 'Word' that is reflected in the first verses of the Bible (Gen 1:1–3): In the beginning, God created the heavens and the earth. And the Creator began this creation with a spoken word, 'And God said [Let there be light].'"[8]

One can then draw a perfect correlation to information because Christians, by faith, believe that the universe was formed by God's *Word* so that what is seen is not made out of that which

---

4. Flew, *There is a God*, 74–75.
5. Lennox, *God's Undertaker*, 177.
6. Lennox, *God's Undertaker*, 177.
7. Lennox, *God's Undertaker*, 177.
8. Lennox, *God's Undertaker*, 177.

is visible.[9] This directly parallels what we know about information; that the carrier of information is visible, yet the information itself is invisible.[10]

6.1 Ramifications of Neo-Darwinism

Looking back at the conclusions that neo-Darwinists elicit to overcome these evidences, one can see that there is an "unwillingness to follow the evidence where it leads simply because one does not like the implications of so doing."[11] This is because what people believe about the genesis and mechanism of life can significantly influence how they live their lives. Stephen Meyer puts it this way: "Whatever theory we adopt has larger philosophical, religious, or worldview implications."[12]

This is very important; notice how a materialistic worldview shapes Dawkins' philosophy of life:

> In a universe of blind physical forces and genetic replication, some people are going to get hurt, other people are going to get lucky, and you won't find any rhyme or reason in it, nor any justice. The universe we observe has precisely the properties we should expect if there is, at bottom, no design, no purpose, no evil and no good, nothing but blind, pitiless indifference.[13]

If we all are just pond scum evolved to a higher order, then Richard Dawkins' statement is quite correct. The predicament is, however, that this is consistent with nihilism, which can be used to justify social Darwinism or even worse. It may not be a coincidence that in one of the Columbine shooters' journals (that of Eric Harris), he said, "People that only know stupid facts that aren't important should be shot, what f****** use are they. NATURAL

---

9. Lennox, *God's Undertaker*, 178.
10. Lennox, *God's Undertaker*, 178.
11. Lennox, *God's Undertaker*, 182.
12. Meyer, *Darwin's Doubt*, 408.
13. Dawkins and Ward, *River out of Eden*, 134.

SELECTION. KILL all retards, people w/ brain f*** ups, drug addicts, people can't figure out to use a f****** lighter."[14]

It is not being suggested that the teaching of natural selection is the ultimate cause of the horrendous Columbine shooting. Still, it is evident from the quotation above that the concept of natural selection could have had an influence on this troubled youth. His choices could have been intellectually justified based on neo-Darwinian philosophy. The same goes for other horrendous acts like social cleansing or social engineering. The ends do not always justify the means, even with the backing of "science."

Eugenics was thought to aid in evolutionary advancement by sterilizing the feeble-minded.[15] In fact, Michael Egnor notes that the physicians who are aware of twentieth-century medicine harbor "bad feelings" towards Darwinism because of eugenics.[16] It was the darkest chapter of American medicine, with over 50,000 people being involuntarily sterilized.[17]

Even worse, it appears to be evident that Hitler's Nazism was influenced by Darwinian theory. This is not to say that Hitler was overtly a Darwinist, but that there were Darwinian implications used to justify Nazism that in fact are consistent with Darwinian views. Note the opening words of what Hitler once said in a private speech to military officers in June 1944:[18]

> War belongs to those events that are essentially unalterable, that remain the same throughout all times, and only change in their form and means. Nature teaches us with every insight into its functioning and its occurrences that the principle of selection rules over it, that the stronger remains victor and the weaker succumbs. It teaches us that what often appears to an individual as brutality, because he himself is affected or because through his education he has turned away from the laws of nature, is

14. Shepard, "Eric Harris' Writing."
15. Stein, *Expelled*.
16. Egnor, *Expelled*.
17. Egnor, *Expelled*.
18. Weikart, *Hitler's Ethic*, 175.

nonetheless fundamentally necessary, in order to bring about a higher evolution of living organisms.[19]

Additionally, Otto Wagener, who had close contact with Hitler before losing favor in mid-1933, recalled a conversation with Hitler in the summer of 1931, where Hitler discussed his enthusiasm for eugenics.[20] According to Wagener, Hitler stated:

> Everywhere in life only a process of selection can prevail. Among the animals, among plants, wherever observations have been made, basically the stronger, the better survives. The simpler life forms have no written constitution. Selection therefore runs a natural course. As Darwin correctly proved: the choice is not made by some agency—nature chooses.[21]

Now, one may object and argue that virtues for sustaining a community will actually aid natural selection rather than hinder it—meaning that doing the evil deeds of eugenics, Nazism, and school shootings cannot be intellectually justified by neo-Darwinism. However, Darwin himself seemed to disagree. In *The Descent of Man*, Darwin said:

> It seems scarcely possible (bearing in mind that we are not here speaking of one tribe being victorious over another) that the number of men gifted with such virtues [sympathy, benevolence, selflessness, bravery], or that the standard of their excellence, could be increased through natural selection, that is, by the survival of the fittest.[22]

Again, this is not to say that Darwinism is a sufficient condition for things like school shootings, eugenics, or Nazism; however, it is undoubtedly a necessary condition.[23] Evidentially, bad science can cause bad consequences.

19. Weikart, *Hitler's Ethic*, 175.
20. Weikart, *Hitler's Ethic*, 185.
21. Wagener and Hein, "Economic Policy Conferences," 40.
22. Darwin, *Descent of Man*, 163.
23. Berlinski, *Expelled*.

6.2 Copernicus and a Scientific Revolution

Good science notes the discrepancies and moves forward regardless of one's religious or political view—no matter how uncomfortable it may make someone. To obtain objective truth, one must be willing to admit error in pursuit. When the evidence seems to contradict a scientific paradigm, then a scientific revolution is appropriate. This is exactly what happened with Copernicus and his heliocentric model for the solar system. What is interesting is that it was the religious crowd who was against this paradigm shift because the former geocentric model that was proposed by Ptolemy made the earth the center of the solar system with perfect circular planetary orbits.

This would understandably fit the theological viewpoint of that era. If God created humanity in His image, then it makes sense to make the dwelling place of this creation at the center of the universe and for the heavenly bodies to have a complete circular orbit because a circle indicates perfection. Yet, regardless of a theological viewpoint or philosophical bias, the evidence must be sought in a pure manner.

Before Ptolemy, Aristarchus was the first person to propose a heliocentric model in the third century BCE, but it was rejected. In the second century CE, Ptolemy proposed his geocentric model and for over a thousand years, this geocentric model was maintained, but it left many questions unanswered. The biggest problem was the observable retrograde motion of the planets. It looked like the planets would orbit around the earth but then move backward and then forward again. In order to fit in the assumption that the earth was the center of the universe, and the heavenly bodies had a perfectly circular orbit, the notion of the equant and epicycles was elicited to account for this retrograde motion of the planets.[24] These ad hoc hypotheses were created to fit the narrative that God made the earth the center of the universe with the heavenly bodies orbiting in a perfect circle. Still, they did not adequately explain the observable evidence.

24. Timberlake and Wallace, "Moving the Earth," 111.

Some 1300 years later, Copernicus proposed a better explanation for this retrograde motion. Without getting into the deep math and science, Copernicus put the sun in the center with the planets orbiting, elliptically. This had much more explanatory power for the observable retrograde motion of the planets. Yet, with this new scientific paradigm, Copernicus knew that the religious crowd would not like this and that they might even kill him if he published it—hence, why it was published the year that he died from a stroke.

Note that this section does not provide an exhaustive account of the history of heliocentricity but highlights similar principles with the neo-Darwinian paradigm. Back then, the ruling political powers (the Catholic church) pressured social leaders to maintain and defend the geocentric model which seemed to better fit into their theological viewpoint. Ad hoc hypotheses were created to account for the discrepancies, and fear was prevalent among those who found issues or challenged said hypotheses. Thus, the geocentric model was held for over a millennium—despite its problems—but eventually, a paradigm shift was necessary to better address those problems.

Similarly, the atheistic community has set up protocols and prohibitions to protect the neo-Darwinian paradigm—at all costs—despite the evidences against it (and to keep God out of science). As alluded to earlier, there is an intellectual fear among many in the scientific field who see issues with neo-Darwinian theory but are reluctant to say anything about it, lest they be punished for challenging the scientific "sainthood" of Charles Darwin and his theory.

6.3 Final Remarks

To recapitulate, this book has demonstrated that the *a priori* assumptions necessary for neo-Darwinian conclusions are unevidential, unconvincing, and subjectively biased. There is no question on whether Darwin and his contemporaries had intelligent minds or have made tremendous contributions in the field of science. Nor is there any sin in their attempting to answer the perennial questions of how humanity came into existence.

The problem persists with neo-Darwinian compromises or shortcuts concerning proper scientific methodology and the political or philosophical extent of which too many scientific leaders have been willing to go so as to mandate neo-Darwinism as the only theory for the origin of life on earth. Unfortunately, as their conclusions lack proper explanatory power and explanatory scope (due to far too many ad hoc hypotheses), their efforts have ultimately hurt the scientific community and field. Fortunately, as in all scientific eras in history, options remain.

Pontification and politicization of neo-Darwinism—as an *intractable fact*—should be annulled, adjusted, and amended. Moreover, regardless of one's position on the matter, this discussion should (and can only) proceed forward with the virtuous restraints of intellectual honesty, open-mindedness, and gracious curiosity—traditionally and historically employed by the scientific world—in action and enforced as quintessential elements of the best, healthiest, and most beneficial pursuit of scientific methodology.

Bibliography

Axe, Douglas D. "Estimating the Prevalence of Protein Sequences Adopting Functional Enzyme Folds." *Journal of Molecular Biology* 341.5 (August 2004) 1295–1315. https://doi.org/10.1016/j.jmb.2004.06.058.
Bahnsen, Greg. *Presuppositional Apologetics: Stated and Defended.* Powder Springs, Georgia and Nacogdoches: American Vision Press and Covenant Media Press, 2008.
Behe, Michael. *The Edge of Evolution: The Search for the Limits of Darwinism.* New York: Simon & Schuster, 2007.
———. *Darwin's Black Box: The Biochemical Challenge to Evolution.* New York: Free Press, 1996.
———. "Reply to My Critics: A Response to Reviews of Darwin's Black Box: The Biochemical Challenge to Evolution." *Biology & Philosophy* 16.5 (November 2001) 683–707. https://doi.org/10.1023/A:1012268700496.
Berlinski, David. *The Devil's Delusion: Atheism and Its Scientific Pretensions.* 2nd ed. New York: Basic Books, 2009.
Berlinski, David, and David Klinghoffer. *The Deniable Darwin & Other Essays.* Seattle: Discovery Institute, 2009.
Boucher, Sandy C. "Methodological Naturalism in the Sciences." *International Journal for Philosophy of Religion* 88.1 (August 2020) 57–80. https://doi.org/10.1007/s11153-019-09728-9.
Carter, Stacy M., and Miles Little. "Justifying Knowledge, Justifying Method, Taking Action: Epistemologies, Methodologies, and Methods in Qualitative Research." *Qualitative Health Research* 17.10 (December 1, 2007) 1316–28. https://doi.org/10.1177/1049732307306927.
Cartwright, Mark. "Nicolaus Copernicus." *World History Encyclopedia* (2020). https://www.worldhistory.org/Nicolaus_Copernicus/.

BIBLIOGRAPHY

Chambers, Robert. *Vestiges of the Natural History of Creation: Together with Explanations: A Sequel.* 5th ed. Cambridge University Press, 2009. https://doi.org/10.1017/CBO9780511693168.

Chignell, Andrew. "The Ethics of Belief." In *The Stanford Encyclopedia of Philosophy.* Metaphysics Research Lab, Stanford University, 2018.

Clifford, William Kingdon. "The Ethics of Belief." In *The Scientific Basis of Morals and Other Essays*, 101–42. New York: J. Fitzgerlad, 2015.

Collins, Francis S. *The Language of God: A Scientist Presents Evidence for Belief.* New York: Free Press, 2006.

Craig, William Lane. "Classical Apologetics." In *Five Views on Apologetics*, 26–55. Counterpoints. Grand Rapids: Zondervan, 2000.

Darwin, Charles. *On the Origin of Species.* Minneapolis: Lerner, 2017.

———. *The Descent of Man, and Selection in Relation to Sex.* Princeton: Princeton University Press, 1981.

Dávalos, Liliana M., Andrea L. Cirranello, Jonathan H. Geisler, and Nancy B. Simmons. "Understanding Phylogenetic Incongruence: Lessons from Phyllostomid Bats." *Biological Reviews* 87.4 (November 2012) 991–1024. https://doi.org/10.1111/j.1469-185X.2012.00240.x.

Davis, Bob. "How Darwin Failed His Own Test." *Explore God* (2022). https://www.exploregod.com/articles/how-darwin-failed-his-own-test.

Dawkins, Richard. "In Short: Nonfiction." *New York Times* (April 9, 1989). https://www.nytimes.com/1989/04/09/books/in-short-nonfiction.html.

———. *The Blind Watchmaker: Why the Evidence of Evolution Reveals a Universe Without Design.* New York: W. W. Norton & Company, 2015.

Dawkins, Richard, and Lalla Ward. *River out of Eden: A Darwinian View of Life.* New York: Basic Books, 1996.

Degnan, James H., and Noah A. Rosenberg. "Gene Tree Discordance, Phylogenetic Inference and the Multispecies Coalescent." *Trends in Ecology & Evolution* 24.6 (June 2009) 332–40. https://doi.org/10.1016/j.tree.2009.01.009.

Dembski, William A. *No Free Lunch: Why Specified Complexity Cannot Be Purchased without Intelligence.* Lanham: Rowman & Littlefield, 2002.

———. *The Design Inference: Eliminating Chance through Small Probabilities.* Cambridge: Cambridge University Press, 2006. https://doi.org/10.1017/CBO9780511570643.

Dennett, D. C. *Darwin's Dangerous Idea: Evolution and the Meaning of Life.* New York: Simon & Schuster, 2014.

Denton, Michael. *Evolution: A Theory in Crisis.* Bethesda: Adler & Adler, 1986.

———. *Evolution: Still a Theory in Crisis.* Revised edition. Seattle: Discovery Institute, 2016.

Fang, Ferric C., R. Grant Steen, and Arturo Casadevall. "Misconduct Accounts for the Majority of Retracted Scientific Publications." *Proceedings of the National Academy of Sciences of the United States of America* 109.42 (2012): 17028–33. https://doi.org/10.1073/pnas.1212247109.

Flew, Antony. *There Is a God: How the World's Most Notorious Atheist Changed His Mind*. New York: Harper One, 2007.
Geisler, Norman L. *Christian Apologetics*. Grand Rapids: Baker Academic, 2013.
Geisler, Norman L., and Frank Turek. *I Don't Have Enough Faith to Be an Atheist*. Wheaton: Crossway, 2004.
Gitt, Werner. *In the Beginning Was Information*. Bielefeld: Christliche Literatur-Verbreitung, 2001.
Gould, Stephen Jay. *Punctuated Equilibrium*. Cambridge: Belknap Press, 2007.
Gould, Stephen Jay, and Phillip E. Johnson. "Impeaching a Self-Appointed Judge." *Scientific American* 267.1 (1992) 118–21.
Graham Lawton, and Michael Syvanen. "Why Darwin Was Wrong about the Tree of Life." *New Scientist* (2009). https://www.newscientist.com/article/mg20126921-600-why-darwin-was-wrong-about-the-tree-of-life/.
Grassé, Pierre-Paul. Evolution of Living Organisms: Evidence for a New Theory of Transformation. New York: Academic Press, 1977.
Gundry, Stanley N., and Steven B. Cowan, eds. *Five Views on Apologetics*. Grand Rapids: Zondervan, 2000.
Habermas, Gary R. "Evidential Apologetics." In *Five Views on Apologetics*, 92–121. Counterpoints. Grand Rapids: Zondervan, 2000.
Hale, Piers J. *Political Descent: Malthus, Mutualism, and the Politics of Evolution in Victorian England*. Chicago; London: The University of Chicago Press, 2014.
Hitching, Francis. *The Neck of the Giraffe: Where Darwin Went Wrong*. New Haven: Ticknor & Fields, 1982.
Hull, David L., and Malcolm J. Kottler. "Darwinism as a Historical Entity:" In *The Darwinian Heritage*, edited by David Kohn, 773–812. Princeton University Press, 1985.
Huxley, Julian. *Essays of a Humanist*. London: Chatto & Windus, 1964.
Huxley, Thomas Henry. "The Darwin Memorial." In *Collected Essays*, 248–52. Cambridge: Cambridge University Press, 2011. https://doi.org/10.1017/CBO9781139149211.
Johnson, Phillip E. "Introduction." In *Darwinism, Science or Philosophy? Proceedings of a Symposium Entitled "Darwinism, Scientific Inference or Philosophical Preference?"* Richardson: Foundation for Thought and Ethics, 1994.
Greenwood, John D. *The Disappearance of the Social in American Social Psychology*. Britain: Cambridge University Press, 2003. https://doi.org/10.1017/CBO9780511512162
Jones, Jeffrey M. "Confidence in U.S. Institutions Down; Average at New Low." *Gallup* (2022).
Kennedy, James. *Skeptics Answered*. Colorado Springs: Multnomah, 2013.
Kenny, Anthony. *The Five Ways: St Thomas Aquinas' Proofs of God's Existence*. Studies in Ethics and the Philosophy of Religion. New York: Routledge, 1969.

BIBLIOGRAPHY

Koonin, Eugene V. "The Biological Big Bang Model for the Major Transitions in Evolution." *Biology Direct* 2.1 (2007) 21. https://doi.org/10.1186/1745-6150-2-21.

Laland, K., Uller, T., Feldman, M. "Does Evolutionary Theory Need a Rethink?" *Nature* 514 (2014) 161–64. https://doi.org/10.1038/514161a

Lennox, John. *God's Undertaker: Has Science Buried God?* New Updated Edition. Oxford: Lion, 2009.

Lester, Lane P., Raymond G. Bohlin, and V. Elving Anderson. *The Natural Limits to Biological Change*. Dallas: Probe Books: 1989.

Lewontin, Richard. "Billions and Billions of Demons." *The New York Review* (January 9, 1997).

Marx, Karl, and Frederick Engels. *Collected Works*. Vol. 41. Moscow: Progress, 1985.

Mayr, Ernst, and Malcolm J. Kottler. "Darwin's Five Theories of Evolution." In *The Darwinian Heritage*, edited by David Kohn, 755–72. Princeton: Princeton University Press, 1985.

McGrath, Alister. *Darwinism and the Divine: Evolutionary Thought and Natural Theology*. John Wiley & Sons, Ltd, 2011.

McLatchie, Jonathan. *Michael Behe Hasn't Been Refuted on the Flagellum*. Seattle: Discovery Institute, 2011.

Meyer, Steven. *Darwin's Doubt: The Explosive Origin of Animal Life and the Case for Intelligent Design*. Seattle: Harper Collins, 2014.

———. "Laws, Causes, and Facts." In *Darwinism, Science or Philosophy? Proceedings of a Symposium Entitled "Darwinism, Scientific Inference or Philosophical Preference?"* 29–40. Richardson: Foundation for Thought and Ethics, 1994.

Miko, I. "Gregor Mendel and the Principles of Inheritance." *Nature Education* 1.1 (2008) 134.

Mittag, Daniel M. "Evidentialism." In *Internet Encyclopedia of Philosophy*. University of Rochester, 2023.

Moreland, James Porter. *Philosophical Foundations for a Christian Worldview*. 2nd mis. Downer's Grove: IVP, 2017.

Morris, Simon Conway. "The Cambrian 'Explosion' of Metazoans." In *Origination of Organismal Form: Beyond the Gene in Developmental and Evolutionary Biology*, 13–32. The Vienna Series in Theoretical Biology. Cambridge: MIT Press, 2003.

Müller, Gerd. "Homology: The Evolution of Morphological Organization." In *Origination of Organismal Form: Beyond the Gene in Developmental and Evolutionary Biology*, 51–69. The Vienna Series in Theoretical Biology. Cambridge: MIT Press, 2003.

Müller, Gerd B., and Stuart A. Newman, eds. *Origination of Organismal Form: Beyond the Gene in Developmental and Evolutionary Biology*. The Vienna Series in Theoretical Biology. Cambridge: MIT Press, 2003.

Müller, Gerd B., and Stuart A. Newman. "Origination of Organismal Form: Beyond the Gene in Developmental and Evolutionary Biology." *Acta Biotheor* 51 (2003) 237–38. https://doi.org/10.1023/A:1025102424947

Musgrave, Ian. "Evolution of the Bacterial Flagellum." In *Why Intelligent Design Fails: A Scientific Critique of the New Creationism*, 72–84. New Brunswick: Rutgers University Press, 2004.

Orwell, George. *Notes on Nationalism*. Grapevine, 2022.

Plantinga, Alvin. "Methodological Naturalism?" *Perspectives on Science and Christian Faith* (1997) 143–54.

Prindle, David F. *The Politics of Evolution*. New York: Routledge, 2015.

Rubens, Tom. *Politics and Neo-Darwinism and Other Essays*. Exeter: Andrews, 2012.

Ruse, Michael. *A Meaning to Life*. New York: Oxford University Press, 2019.

———. *Charles Darwin*. Hoboken: John Wiley & Sons, 2008.

———. "Darwinism: Philosophical Preference, Scientific Inference, and Good Research Strategy." In *Darwinism, Science or Philosophy? Proceedings of a Symposium Entitled "Darwinism, Scientific Inference or Philosophical Preference?"* Richardson: Foundation for Thought and Ethics, 1994.

Russell, Bertrand. *The Conquest of Happiness*. USA: Signet, 1952.

Sanford, John C. *Genetic Entropy & The Mystery of the Genome: The Genome Is Degenerating*. Lima: Elim, 2005.

Schwabe, Christian. *The Genomic Potential Hypothesis: A Chemist's View of the Origins, Evolution and Unfolding of Life*. Boca Raton: CRC, 2001.

Staddon, John. *Scientific Method: How Science Works, Fails to Work, and Pretends to Work*. New York: Routledge/Taylor & Francis Group, 2018.

Stein, Ben. "Expelled: No Intelligence Allowed," 2008. https://www.youtube.com/watch?v=V5EPymcWp-g&t=30s.

Taros, Trenton, Christopher Zoppo, Nathan Yee, Jack Hanna, and Christine MacGinnis. "Retracted COVID-19 Articles: Significantly More Cited Than Other Articles Within Their Journal of Origin. *Scientometrics* 128.5 (2023) 2935–43. https://doi.org/10.1007%2Fs11192-023-04707-4

Thomas, C. George. *Research Methodology and Scientific Writing*. Second Edition. India: ANE Books, 2021.

Timberlake, Todd, and Paul Wallace. "Moving the Earth: The Revolutions of Copernicus." In *Finding Our Place in the Solar System: The Scientific Story of the Copernican Revolution*. Cambridge University Press.

Wallace, J. Warner, and Lee Strobel. *Cold-Case Christianity (Updated and Expanded Edition): A Homicide Detective Investigates the Claims of the Gospels*. Colorado Springs: David C. Cook, 2023.

Wagener, Otto, and Ruth Hein. "The Economic Policy Conferences Begin— Wagener Presents His Plans for a 'Social Economy'—Hitler Senses the Philosopher's Stone in His Hand." In *Hitler—Memoirs of a Confidant*, edited by Henry Ashby Turner, 39–48. New Haven: Yale University Press, 1985. https://doi.org/10.2307/j.ctt1ww3vv7.11.

Wallace, Alfred. "Sir Charles Lyell on Geological Climates and the Origin of Species." *Quarterly Review* (1869) 359–94.

Wartick, J. W. "The Presuppositional Apologetic of Cornelius Van Til." *Reconstructing Faith* (July 9, 2012).

Weikart, Richard. *Hitler's Ethic*. London: Palgrave Macmillan, 2009.

Whitman, William B., David C. Coleman, and William J. Wiebe. "Prokaryotes: The Unseen Majority." *Proceedings of the National Academy of Sciences* 95.12 (1998) 6578–83. https://doi.org/10.1073/pnas.95.12.6578.

Wilkenfeld, Daniel, and Tania Lombrozo. "Inference to the Best Explanation (IBE) Versus Explaining for the Best Inference (EBI)." *Science and Education* 24.9–10 (2015) 1059–77. https://doi.org/10.1007/s11191-015-9784-4.

Williams, Clifford. *Existential Reasons for Belief in God: A Defense of Desires & Emotions for Faith*. Downers Grove: IVP, 2011.

Willmer, Pat. "Convergence and Homoplasy in the Evolution of Organismal Form." In *Origination of Organismal Form: Beyond the Gene in Developmental and Evolutionary Biology*, 33–49. Cambridge: MIT Press, 2003.

Index

a priori, 1, 2, 4, 13, 41, 50, 53, 61, 69, 72, 73, 91, 92
a priori assumption, xv, 2–4, 6, 10–12, 15, 19, 20, 31, 37–41, 43, 47, 65, 70, 72, 77–79, 84, 90, 91
ad hoc, 38, 39, 77, 78, 92
ad hoc hypotheses, 73, 97–99
aesthetics, 23
agency, 22, 42, 72, 96
Ancient Repetitive Elements (AREs), 17, 18
apobetics, 16, 66–68, 78
apologetics, xv, 79–87, 89
atheism, xvii, 6, 25, 34, 75
Axe, Douglas, 15, 63

Behe, Michael, 21, 22, 24, 54, 55, 56, 64, 90, 91
Berlinski, David, 22, 24, 25, 46, 73, 91
biases, xvii, 10, 46, 73, 77, 78, 90, 91, 97, 98
biology, xvi, 4, 7, 27, 68, 87, 91
Boucher, Sandy, 31, 34, 70, 71, 91

Burgess Shale, 15, 25, 43–46

Cambrian, 8, 26, 46
Cambrian explosion, 15, 30, 44, 45, 50, 77, 91
Cambrian period/era, 8, 14, 22, 25, 30, 34, 46, 47, 50, 65
causality, 20, 22
chance, 15, 16, 22, 29, 59–61, 78, 85, 91
chemistry, 4, 25, 39, 41, 50, 87
Christianity, 6, 80, 81, 84, 89
Christians, xvi, 12, 22, 29, 30, 33, 36, 79–83, 85, 88–91, 93
classical apologetics, 81, 82, 85
Cliffordian principles, 84
Collins, Francis, 9, 17, 21, 22, 53, 90, 91
combinational probability, 62, 63
conditional probability, 64, 65
convergent evolution, 52
Copernicus, Nicolaus, 5, 89, 97, 98
corroborating evidence, 1, 10
Creationism, 22, 36, 53
creed, 19, 22, 31

cumulative selection, 34, 59, 60
cyclical change, 58, 59, 77, 91

Darwin, Charles, 7, 8, 35, 44, 45, 54, 58, 88, 98
Darwin's finches, 10, 58
Darwinism, 7, 9, 15, 18, 19, 24, 30–32, 35
data, ix–xii, 4, 12, 20, 35–38, 40, 41, 43, 47, 53, 77, 81, 87
Dawkins, Richard, xvii, 18, 24, 27, 28, 30, 34, 38, 42, 46, 48, 59–62, 65, 73, 76, 87, 88, 91, 92, 94
deductive reasoning, 2
Dembski, William, 15, 22, 29, 55, 56, 90
Dennett, Daniel, 28, 29, 34, 42, 48
Denton, Michael, 51, 52
design inference, 15, 16, 22, 32, 72
Divine foot, 14, 19, 31, 34, 73, 78, 92
DNA, 14–16, 22, 51, 61–65, 67, 69, 78, 91, 92
dogma, 19, 22, 24, 72
Drosophila fruit flies, 58

empirical evidence, 7, 10, 38, 47, 52, 53, 59, 84, 85
empirical facts, 2, 42, 46
epistemic humility, xvii
Escherichia coli, 57
Eugenics, 95, 96
evidential apologetics, 82
evidentialism, 79, 81, 83, 84
  strict evidentialism, 83, 84
evolutionary assumption, 10, 38, 53, 59, 77, 85, 91
explanatory power, 5, 10, 34, 38, 39, 41, 98, 99
explanatory scope, 34, 38, 39, 99

faith, 5–7, 13, 17, 19, 20, 72, 78–80, 86, 93
falsifiability, 4, 38

falsification, 19
five a priori assumptions of neo-Darwinism, 10, 35, 37–39, 77
five levels of information, 66, 68
flagella/flagellum, 56, 57
Flew, Antony, 92
forensic science, 9, 20, 43, 71, 72
fossil record, 8, 14, 25, 29, 43, 45, 46, 50, 85

Geisler, Norman, 20, 22, 70, 90
genetics, 8, 18, 25, 26
  genetic code, 48, 51
  genetic commonalities, 51
  genetic entropy, 16, 22, 61
  genetic limits, 57, 58, 77, 91
  genetic mutations, 10, 25, 28, 34, 50, 57, 58, 61, 78
genome, 16, 17, 26, 52, 61, 63, 65
  genomic potential hypothesis, 25, 50
geo-centricity, 5
Gitt, Werner, 16, 17, 19, 22, 28, 41, 67
God, 6, 9, 17–19, 23, 29, 31, 33, 75, 76, 79–83, 86–89, 92, 93, 97, 98
Gould, Stephen Jay, 30, 38, 46, 85, 91
gradualism, 10, 15, 21, 30, 44–47, 77, 85

heliocentricity, 97, 98
homology, 26, 27, 52
Huxley, Julian, 32–34, 75, 87
hypothesis, 5, 24, 25, 37, 42, 43, 46, 88

ideology, 19, 21, 22, 33, 87
induction, 14, 20, 22, 41
  inductive theory, 2
inference, xvii, 2, 15, 22, 32, 72, 85

INDEX

information and the mind, 14, 65–67, 69, 72, 78, 91, 93
intellectual honesty, xvii, 99
Intelligent Design, 16, 24, 32, 36, 39, 65, 72, 77, 78, 88, 92
irreducible complexity, 21, 53, 54, 57

junk DNA, 17

Koonin, Eugene, 49

lawn of life, 25, 50
laws of logic, 20, 41, 43, 91
laws of nature, 4–6, 41, 43, 72, 91, 95
Lennox, John, 12, 16, 19, 22, 88, 90, 93
Lewontin, Richard, 13, 31, 34, 72, 76, 91, 92

Marx, Karl, 75
materialism, 14, 19, 72, 73
mathematics, 3, 4, 15, 16, 41, 42
Mayr, Ernst, 29, 34, 42
McGrath, Alister, 9, 18–20, 22, 27, 42, 91
McLatchie, Jonathan, 57
methinks, 28, 59, 60
methodological naturalism, 10, 13, 14, 19, 20, 22, 31, 32, 38, 70, 72
methodology, 35, 79, 80, 81, 82, 85
methods, x, 13, 31, 73, 79, 80, 89
Meyer, Stephen, 14–16, 19, 20, 24, 25, 28, 41, 42, 45, 46, 48, 72, 94
mind, 14, 16, 22, 23, 65–67, 69, 72, 78, 91, 93
Modern Evolutionary Synthesis, 9
morphology, 30
Morris, Simon Conway, 25, 26, 45, 47, 91
Müller, Gerd, 25–27, 30, 43, 45, 91

Nagel, Thomas, 23–25, 27, 28, 32, 91
natural selection, 7, 9, 24, 25, 27, 29, 30, 44, 50, 57–59, 75, 90, 95, 96
Nazism, 95, 96
neo-Darwinian conclusions, 3, 7, 8, 9, 12, 15, 20, 33, 35, 39, 40, 58, 77, 90, 91, 98, 99
neo-Darwinism, xv–xvii, 3, 7, 9, 10, 11, 24, 40, 42, 43, 79, 84, 85, 87
Newman, Stuart, 25
Newton's Universal Law of Gravitation, 41
Nihilism, xvii, 94

On the Origin of Species, 7, 8, 26, 30, 45, 58, 74, 88
origin mechanism of life, xvii, 9
origin of life, 1, 14, 20, 23, 43, 71, 87, 88, 92, 99
orogeny, 71

paradigm, 5, 97, 98
philosophical principles, 4
philosophy, 10, 29, 42, 71, 94
physics, 3, 4, 6, 39, 41, 42
Plantinga, Alvin, 19, 20, 22, 31, 90
postmodern scientism, xv
postmodern world, 3
pragmatics, 16, 66–68, 78
presupposition, xv, xvii, 1, 2, 7, 19, 21, 69, 79–81, 87, 88
presuppositionalism, 80
Principle of Uniformity, 6, 7, 20
Prindle, David, 53, 76
probabilistic resources, 64, 65
probability, ix, 23, 63, 64, 65
probability theory, 78, 85
punctuated equilibrium, 30, 38, 46, 47, 77
punctuation, 46, 47, 85

INDEX

qualitative science, 4, 39, 40, 41, 42, 43, 47, 91
quantitative science, 3, 4, 40–43

ramifications, 39, 89, 94
Ruse, Michael, 27, 29, 32, 34, 49, 57, 91

Sanford, John C., 16, 22, 28, 61
Schwabe, Christian, 25, 50, 91
scientific fact, xvi, 3, 13, 15, 21, 27, 77
scientific method, 6, 13, 19, 20, 37, 39, 43, 78, 89, 99
semantics, 16, 66, 68
stasis, 30, 34, 46, 47
statistics, ix, 16, 66, 68
Stein, Ben, 87, 88
supernatural, 31, 32, 34, 70–72
syntax, 16, 66, 68

theism, 36, 82, 83, 92
theistic evolutionist 9, 12, 17, 18, 36, 91
theorem, 5, 20
theory, 41, 42, 43, 47, 89
time and chance, 10, 15, 16, 22, 38, 59, 62, 65, 72, 77, 78, 91, 93
tree of life hypothesis, 10, 25, 38, 43, 47, 49, 51, 77, 91
Turek, Frank, 20, 21, 22, 70

unscientific, 7, 13, 19, 22, 32, 84

Walcott, Charles Doolittle, 44
Wallace, Alfred, 7, 8, 35, 73
Willmer, Pat, 25, 26, 52, 53, 91
worldview, 5, 6, 12, 22, 25, 33, 34, 85, 88, 89, 90, 94

www.ingramcontent.com/pod-product-compliance
Lightning Source LLC
Chambersburg PA
CBHW050836160426
43192CB00010B/2044